# The Complete
# Will Kit

# The Complete Will Kit

## SECOND EDITION

**F. Bruce Gentry**

**Jens C. Appel III**

JOHN WILEY & SONS, INC.

New York • Chichester • Brisbane • Toronto • Singapore • Weinheim

Copyright © 1997 by F. Bruce Gentry and Jens C. Appel III
Published by John Wiley & Sons, Inc.

This publication is designed to provide accurate and authoritative
information in regard to the subject matter covered. It is sold with
the understanding that the publisher is not engaged in rendering legal,
accounting, or other professional services. If legal advice or other expert
assistance is required, the services of a competent professional person
should be sought.

*Library of Congress Cataloging-in-Publication Data:*

Gentry, F. Bruce, 1946–
       The complete will kit / F. Bruce Gentry, Jens C. Appel III.—
    2nd ed.
          p.   cm.
       Includes index.
       ISBN 0-471-14138-0 (cloth : alk. paper).—ISBN 0-471-14137-2
    (pbk. : alk. paper)
       1. Wills—United States—Popular works.   2. Executors and
    administrators—United States—Popular works.   3. Estate planning—
    United States—Popular works.   I. Appel, Jens C., 1948–   .
    KF755.Z9A45   1996
    346.7305'4—dc20
    [347.30654]                                            96-21975

Printed in the United States of America

10 9 8 7 6 5 4 3 2 1

This book is dedicated to our parents:


William James Gentry, Sr.
Virginia Reese Gentry


J. C. Appel
Elizabeth Chitwood Appel

# *Preface*

Estate planning and the need for a valid will has become increasingly important in today's complex world. A valid will allows you to direct the way your estate is distributed, and can help avoid unnecessary expense and delay in probate. A valid will can also help your family avoid the confusion and stress that can result from lack of instructions regarding your estate. A valid Last Will and Testament, so often overlooked, can prove to be the most generous gift you leave to your family and loved ones.

This book is intended for those who are concerned with life, its riches, rewards, and realities. Now—as you read this book—you have the opportunity to prepare an estate plan and execute a valid will. Later—the time most people set aside to write a will—is often too late.

Writing a will should be viewed as a part of responsible living. From the time you enter adulthood, and throughout your life, a valid will should be a part of your estate plan. As your life and estate change you may change your will to meet your needs. Writing a will is a simple procedure that can be easily repeated whenever necessary. Because personal, family, and estate situations change over time, your first will is seldom your last.

This book serves as a guide to the process of preparing a valid will and includes the basic information you need, along with worksheets for estate inventory, Executor data, and other information you will find useful in organizing your estate. A complete set of detachable will forms and related documents are provided for your convenience. Your will may be as long, or short, as necessary to express your estate plan. In the early stages of adult life your estate plan may be simple and your will brief. As time goes by you may require a lengthy document to direct specific bequests to children, grandchildren, relatives, and charities, or to include other provisions. The will forms included in the Document Set offer both single- and multiple-page formats. Also included are Self-Proving forms, Codicil forms, and forms for a Letter of Instructions. All forms are perforated so that they may be easily detached.

The Executor's Guide (Chapter 6) includes information that can be helpful in preparing a will, and may also be useful if you are named Executor of another's estate. The task of the Executor is critical to the efficient, and effective, administration of the estate. The Executor's Guide can help you make informed decisions regarding this important role in your estate plan.

Chapter 8, on Living Wills, includes fundamental information and lists a number of resources that can provide invaluable assistance. *The Complete Will Kit* can be of great value even if you require professional assistance in formulating and executing your estate plan. The basic knowledge gained from this book should allow you to make informed decisions regarding your estate plan, and the worksheets can help you to organize important personal information. Preparation and organization will help you use professional time wisely and effectively.

Be sure to read the entire book before preparing your estate plan or will. The text may make you aware of situations that affect your plans, or you may be alerted to alternate estate planning methods that answer your needs. The right, and responsibility, to plan and direct your estate is yours; only inaction can deny you the chance.

F. BRUCE GENTRY

*Salem, Virginia*

# Acknowledgments

I would like to thank all those who helped in the process of preparing this manuscript, with particular thanks due to a special friend and associate, Sue Amos, who allowed me the time to write by managing my business responsibilities, and to Ashley Wainwright, who helped with the research. I also wish to thank my wife Amelia and daughters, Amy and Morgen, and our family dog, Max, for their continuing support and encouragement. And finally, a special mention, just because he deserves it, goes to John Adrian Sims Rutherford.

F. BRUCE GENTRY

# Contents

## CHAPTER 2 *Writing Your Will* 21

## CHAPTER 3 *Your Property* 31

# The Complete
# Will Kit

# Introduction

*The Complete Will Kit* has been used by tens of thousands of Americans as a guide to the process of writing a will and maintaining a current estate plan. The simple act of writing a will can help your family avoid emotional distress and uncertainty, and prevent unnecessary expense to your estate as well. The process of preparing a valid will, once learned, can be used throughout your adult lifetime as you update or revise your estate plan. This second edition continues to provide the basic information necessary to prepare and update your estate plan, along with timely information regarding Living Wills and Powers of Attorney, two important estate planning concerns in this day of rapidly advancing technology and changing attitudes concerning individual rights to limit medical treatment in terminal situations.

Every effort has been made to provide current information regarding the specific state requirements throughout the United States for preparing a valid will and related documents. Although there are some minor variances among states regarding the requirements involved in executing a Last Will and Testament, the form, and formalities, of a valid will have long been established and are similar in all states. Executing a Living Will or Power of Attorney may require you to seek further assistance through appropriate public or private agencies. Many state laws respecting Living Wills are fairly new (legally speaking), and forms, formalities, and procedures differ. Appropriate state forms and additional information concerning Living Wills and Powers of Attorney, and individual state requirements connected with those documents are widely available. Chapter 8 contains a directory of state and national resources that can provide forms and current information for your state. The reader should be attentive to current state law and policies relating to these issues.

## About the Book

The purpose of *The Complete Will Kit, Second Edition*, is to provide the reader with a basic knowledge of estate planning and serve as an action guide to the process of writing a will. This new edition contains new sections on Living Wills, Powers of Attorney, and a comprehensive guide to legal resources for all fifty states. State requirements have also been updated.

Simple, direct language is used, and words that may be unfamiliar are explained in the text and defined in the Glossary. Gender-neutral terms like "Executor" are used for those words that also have a specifically feminine form, such as "Executrix." Samples are used extensively throughout the text, and common estate planning concerns are illustrated in a series of sample wills based on the experiences of four generations of the fictitious Light family.

The Executor's Guide, with its step-by-step explanation of how to settle an estate, removes the mystery from the probate process. A series of Estate Inventory sheets is included in the Record Set for your convenience. Detachable Executor Data sheets provide space to list information needed to settle an estate. A working knowledge of the process of settling an estate and estate taxes helps you plan effectively.

The remainder of this Introduction is a brief orientation to the components of a simple will.

## Sample Will

A will is simply a document, signed before two (or more) witnesses, that records your intent for the distribution of your estate. Such a will is known as a testamentary will and is recognized in all 50 states and the District of Columbia. The people involved with a testamentary will are as follows:

**Testator.** A person who writes a valid will is called a Testator. A will identifies the Testator by his or her full name and legal address. The Testator executes a will by signing and dating the document in front of witnesses.

**Executor.** Your will names an Executor for your estate and empowers him or her to act for you. This person will be responsible for administering the estate and carrying out the provisions of your will.

**Beneficiary.** The person or organization you name to receive all, or a portion, of your estate is known as a beneficiary. For clarity, each beneficiary should be identified by full name and relationship.

**Witnesses.** Witnesses are persons who together see the Testator sign and date a will and who then sign the will at the Testator's request. Witnesses should be persons who are not related to the Testator and who are not mentioned in the will. Witnesses must be adults and should list their addresses when signing.

In the following sample will (Figures 1 and 2), a 58-year-old man leaves his entire estate to his wife, except for three specific bequests to his son, daughter, and church. He has also included a provision specifying that if his wife does not survive him, his estate is to be divided equally between his children. The will was executed in 1930, with two of his neighbors as witnesses. Basic components of this sample will are keyed alphabetically to brief explanations.

# LAST WILL AND TESTAMENT

(A) I, _____Paul Samuel Light_____ , resident

of the __County__ of __Botetourt__ in the State of __VIRGINIA__ ,

(B) being of sound mind, do make and declare the following to be my LAST WILL AND TESTAMENT and expressly revoke all my prior wills and codicils and certify that I am not acting under undue influence, duress or menace.

## I. EXECUTOR

(C) I appoint _____Naomi Lee Spencer Light, my wife,__ EXECUTOR of this my LAST WILL AND TESTAMENT. If this EXECUTOR is unable to serve for any reason,

(D) then I appoint _____Carroll Abraham Light, my son,_____ EXECUTOR.

(E) The EXECUTOR is empowered to carry out all provisions of this WILL.
The EXECUTOR shall have all statutory powers available under State law.

(F) The EXECUTOR named shall not be required to post surety bond. I direct that no outside appraisal be made of my estate, unless required for estate tax purposes.

## II. BEQUESTS

(G) I give my entire estate to my beloved wife, Naomi Lee Spencer Light, with the exception of the following three bequests.

(H) 1. To my son, Carroll Abraham Light, I give my Parker 12 gauge shotgun.

(H) 2. To my daughter, Mary Alice Light, I give the sum of two hundred dollars ($200.00).

(I) 3. To my church, Brandy Run Church of God, I give the sum of fifty dollars ($50.00).

(J) If my wife, Naomi Lee Spencer Light, should die before me, then all of my estate, except for the above bequests, I give to my son, Carroll Abraham Light and my daughter, Mary Alice Light, in equal shares.

(K) This concludes my entire Last Will and Testament.

*Figure 1*

# Last Will and Testament

**(A)** A will sets out the full legal name of the Testator and identifies the jurisdiction of legal residence (city or county and state).

**(B)** A statement that the Testator is of sound mind and free of outside influence. All previous wills and codicils are declared to be void.

## I. EXECUTOR

**(C)** An Executor, identified by full legal name and relationship, is named to settle the estate.

**(D)** An alternate Executor is named, again identified by full legal name and relationship.

**(E)** Powers are granted to the Executor to carry out provisions of the will.

**(F)** To save expenses to the estate, the Testator directs that no surety bond be required of the Executor and that no outside appraisals of the estate be made.

## II. BEQUESTS

**(G)** The entire estate is left to the primary beneficiary, identified by full legal name and relationship, except for three specific bequests.

**(H)** Personal property bequests are specific, and beneficiaries are identified by full legal name and relationship.

**(I)** A specific charitable bequest clearly identifies the organization that is to receive it.

**(J)** A provision is included specifying how to dispose of the estate if the primary beneficiary dies first.

**(K)** To safeguard against additions, a statement indicates the end of the entire will.

## III. WITNESSED

**(L)** The Testator must date and sign the will in the presence of all the witnesses together.

**(M)** The will is identified by the name of the Testator and the date.

**(N)** Witnesses sign the will using full legal names and listing their addresses. Witnesses should be adults not mentioned in the will.

IN WITNESS WHEREOF, I have hereunto set my hand this *twenty-ninth* day

(L)  of *October* , 19 **30** .

*Paul Samuel Light*
(Testator signature)

# III. WITNESSED

(M)  This LAST WILL AND TESTAMENT of *Paul Samuel Light* was signed and declared to be his/~~her~~ LAST WILL AND TESTAMENT in our presence at his/~~her~~ request and in his/~~her~~ presence and the presence of each other as witnesses this *twenty-seventh*

day of *October* , 19 **30** .

(N)  *James Robert Sawyer* Rt. 1, Box 293, Springwood, VA.
(Witness signature) (Address)

(N)  *Ellen Susan Sawyer* - Rt. 1, Box 293, Springwood, VA
(Witness signature) (Address)

_____ _____
(Witness signature) (Address)

*Figure 2*

As the preceding sample shows, even a brief will can be complete and effective. To be legally valid, a testamentary will must be properly witnessed. This simple procedure is outlined as follows:

### Correct Witness Procedure

1. Have your witnesses together when you are ready to sign your will.
2. Sign and date your will in front of both (or all three) witnesses. (You may cover the contents for privacy, if desired.)
3. Have each witness, in the presence of you and of one another, sign the will and list his or her address.

Your witnesses should be "disinterested," that is, people who are not mentioned in the will and who are not related to you. When you sign (execute) your will, you must do so in front of all your witnesses together. Two adult witnesses are required everywhere in the United States except Louisiana and Vermont, where three witnesses are required. The witnesses verify that you signed your will in their presence and were of sound mind and not acting under the influence of others.

Additional information about estate planning, trusts, and financial planning is available at your local library and bookstores. The local probate court, law libraries, and state taxation departments can all be of assistance and are good sources of current, specific information.

If you decide that you need further professional assistance in preparing your will, be sure to fill out the inventory and data forms and prepare a draft copy of your will. Having your plans outlined and complete estate information available can save time, expense, and error. Most important, such advance planning can ensure that your will expresses an informed and clearly thought out distribution of your property that omits nothing and leaves nothing to chance.

CHAPTER *1*

---

# *Preparing Your Estate Plan*

## *The Role of Your Will*

Estate planning involves the creation, conservation, and eventual distribution of your real and personal property. Although there are other methods that can transfer ownership of estate assets, a valid will remains a cornerstone of effective estate planning. Many estate planning techniques are in common use that allow property to pass outside the probate system. Joint titling of both real and personal assets, gifts, trusts, and other methods of distribution that avoid probate and taxes are common estate planning measures. The role of your will in estate planning is flexible, addressing your personal needs at various stages of your life and setting out your plan for the assets and property not disposed of by other means. Naming an Executor for your estate, specifying guardians for children, or making a gift of a personal treasure to a close friend are typical choices expressed in a will. No matter how extensively you've arranged your estate plan, never neglect the need for a valid will.

As shown by the sample in the Introduction, your will can be a very simple document, setting out your complete plan regarding distribution of your estate. Your will should always reflect your current goals, family needs, and personal decisions. Your will can be amended or revoked and replaced by a new one at any time.

## Estate Concerns

You may reasonably expect to write several wills in a lifetime. The process of writing, executing, and maintaining a will should become a routine part of your overall estate plan. Updating your will as needed can help keep it simple, effective, and responsive to your current needs.

The passage of time can make significant changes in your personal, family, and estate situation. The legal responsibilities of property ownership and personal liability begin with adulthood and continue throughout your lifetime. The process of estate planning often begins early with the purchase of life insurance and the execution of a simple will. Your first will, often simple in content, may be supplemented, or supplanted, to take into account guardians, additional beneficiaries, charitable bequests, or other elements of your estate plan. Consider your estate, beneficiaries, and family needs, and plan accordingly when deciding on the content of your will. Bequests and provisions in your will may be as brief or extensive as needed to express your wishes and plans. A simple will is not necessarily brief.

Assessing your personal situation is a task you are best qualified to perform. Typical concerns include your health, marital situation, and dependents; the status of your beneficiaries; and the risks involved in your daily life. Your age and health, and that of your beneficiaries, is extremely important in shaping your estate plan. At the early stages of adult life, your assets and responsibilities may be few, requiring only a simple will to transfer your estate to your beneficiaries. At such times, your primary concern may be to assure that your personal property is disposed of in the manner you decide. Automobiles, household goods, jewelry, and electronic, photographic, hobby, or sports equipment may be disposed of in a valid will with little extended planning required. In later years, after a lifetime of changes, the same concerns often apply. The estate planning cycle often begins, and ends, with a simple will.

Changes in your estate plan usually follow important events in your life, including:

- Moving.
- Marriage.
- Birth or adoption of children.
- Divorce.
- Remarriage.

- Death of grandparents and others of their generation.
- Maturity of children.
- Birth of grandchildren.
- Death of parents and others of their generation.
- Growth of estate, including inheritance(s).
- Need for estate tax planning.
- Continuing health care needs.
- Death of spouse.
- Death of beneficiaries.

These events can affect the nature of your estate and influence your choice of beneficiaries. Be sure to review your estate plan periodically and address important events that change your estate planning goals and methods.

# Special Situations

Basic provisions in your will can adequately address many of the special situations listed in the preceding section. Other estate planning methods, especially trusts, may also be considered in certain situations. As changes occur, your will, along with the other components of your estate plan, should be kept current.

## MARRIAGE

Marriage can affect your personal goals, the ownership of property, and your estate plan. Your will, and your spouse's, should address your shared and individual goals. The need for a will is especially critical if you intend your spouse to inherit the majority of your estate. In most states, if there is no will to direct otherwise, your spouse may inherit only a portion of your assets. Also, be aware that all states allow a spouse the right of "elective share." This simply means that your spouse may elect to take the portion of the estate left in your will or an amount defined by state law. Because of the elective share laws, it is virtually impossible to disinherit your legal spouse totally. At all times in married life, each spouse should have a will to express current estate planning goals.

Marriage, of course, has a significant effect on property ownership. In community-property states, each spouse has a one-half interest in all property of the marriage. The property interest of each spouse is individual and, if no other plans are made, should be disposed of in the will. Property owned individually before the marriage remains separate and may also be distributed in a will. If you live in a community-property state, be sure your will specifies how you intend to dispose of the individual property that is a part of your estate. You and your spouse should coordinate your estate plans, and each of you should prepare wills accordingly.

*JOINT OWNERSHIP / RIGHT OF SURVIVORSHIP.* Joint ownership, with right of survivorship, is a common estate planning technique used by married couples, as well as by others who own property together. Property held in joint ownership transfers title to the survivor upon the death of one of the owners. This type of transfer is automatic and avoids probate of the property. Real estate, bank accounts, and other property are often jointly titled by couples as an estate planning measure. Be sure to review deeds, titles, and account agreements that are titled jointly to ensure that "right of survivorship" is included. Joint owners may plan for the remote possibility of simultaneous death by naming an alternate beneficiary in their wills. If both partners die together and their wills agree on an alternate beneficiary, that person will receive the property once held jointly by both. For this reason, it is extremely important that spouses' wills agree on major provisions, especially the choice of alternate beneficiaries and Executor. In some states, a form of real property ownership, "tenants by the entirety," is available to married couples only. This type of ownership also transfers title automatically to the remaining spouse.

*TRUSTS AND LIFE ESTATES.* Trusts and life estates are options that can offer many advantages and may be considered as part of your estate plan. Trusts are often used to provide income to a surviving spouse or other beneficiaries while the assets of the trust are conserved for future distribution. There are several types of trusts and methods of establishing them to achieve different purposes. You and your spouse should discuss your goals, tax position, and anticipated income needs when considering trusts. A life estate can guarantee your spouse or other beneficiary the right to occupy real property, such as a house or farm, while allowing the title to be transferred to another beneficiary. Title transfers prior to death avoid probate and, because a life estate is a liability against real property, may lower the value of the taxable estate.

*DIVORCE / REMARRIAGE / OTHER RELATIONSHIPS.* Divorce and remarriage can be of special concern to those preparing an estate plan. If you or your spouse have been married previously, be sure to check for accuracy all titles, deeds, and insurance policies acquired during the previous marriage. If either spouse has children by a previous marriage, choices must be made regarding their place, if any, in your estate plan. For those who are married, agreement and coordination are essential to effective estate planning.

Relationships other than marriage may also affect your estate planning decisions. In some states, those who live together continuously for a period of time may be considered legally married, even though no formal marriage ceremony has taken place. Common-law marriages of this type may have significant impact on the way an estate is divided. If you or one of your beneficiaries maintains a living relationship with someone who is not a legal spouse, you should consider the implications carefully. States that currently recognize common-law marriage are Alabama, Colorado, Georgia, Idaho, Iowa, Kansas, Montana, Ohio, Oklahoma, Pennsylvania, Rhode Island, South Carolina, and Texas. The District of Columbia also recognizes common-law marriages.

In summary, those who are currently married, considering marriage, or maintaining a relationship that could have the legal status of marriage should take special care when preparing an estate plan. Each spouse should have a will, and the major provisions should not conflict or disagree. Spouses who have named each other as sole or primary beneficiary should always name alternates to receive the estate if both die simultaneously.

## CHILDREN AND DEPENDENTS

If you are responsible for the care of minor children, you should nominate a guardian for them in your will. While your wishes are not strictly binding, the probate court usually appoints your nominee as guardian when you express your intent in your will. Designating a person to serve as guardian of minor children in the case of the simultaneous death of both parents is important, and the wills of both parents should agree regarding the designation of the contingent guardian. Close family members, including the spouse and extended family, are usually relied on to provide care for minor children until they reach maturity. A healthy surviving spouse, provided with adequate financial resources through insurance or estate assets, is usually the best choice for dependent care. If you are single or lack family resources, the importance of this type of planning becomes more critical.

Plans for dependents, especially intentions regarding care, education, religious affiliation, and management of assets, should be outlined and discussed with your chosen guardian. The guardian you appoint must consent and be acceptable to the court. Financial support, especially over a long period of time, may require a trust or other arrangements.

● **Example** ────────────────────────────────

If my wife, Jo Anne Stone Light, does not survive me by more than 180 days, then I give my entire estate to my daughter, Linda Lee Light, and my son, Paul Abraham Light, in equal shares, and I appoint Abraham Lee Light, my father, as guardian of my children until they attain their majority.

────────────────────────────────●

## CHILDREN: UNEQUAL SHARES

If you have no will, your children—minor and/or adult, biological and/or adopted, legitimate and/or illegitimate—may have an equal claim on your estate. Most states also provide your unborn (pretermitted) children a share of your estate if you die intestate. Often, parents have children with unequal needs or have concerns about the ability of a particular child to manage assets. In later stages of estate planning, prior gifts made to children may affect the terms of your will. Providing for children requires special care as you out-line your estate plan. When children are minors or require continuing care, you may consider estate planning methods beyond your will that provide in-come and financial security over time. If you have minor or adult children that you intend to exclude from your estate or treat differently in your will, take special care to spell out your intentions.

Your will may include special instructions regarding property left to mi-nors. You may specify a person to hold and care for gifts of property to those who are immature or, by law, unable to take possession.

● **Example**

I direct my son, Frederick Roger Hale, who is my appointed Executor, to keep the Browning shotgun, SN 67890, that I have given to my grandson, Charles James Hale, until he has reached maturity and is able to safely assume possession, or reaches the age of 18 years.

If you plan to exclude a particular child from your estate, be sure to state that intention in your will. If you fail to mention one child while leaving gifts to others, the court may rule that you simply overlooked that child and may award him or her a share proportionate to those of your other children. Be sure provisions regarding children are clear, complete, and direct.

● **Example**

I have purposely made no provision for my son, William Samuel Stull, because I have neither seen him nor heard from him in the last thirty years.

Be sure to list the reasons for unequal treatment of your children in your will. Unequal division of your estate can often result from prior gifts or loans made to your children.

● **Example**

I give my entire estate to my son, James Carl Stull. I have intentionally made no provi-sion for my other son, Howard Charles Stull, since I previously purchased an eighty-acre farm in Pasco County, Florida, for him in accordance with his expressed wishes.

Making unequal provisions in your will should always be planned care-fully. Children who are treated unequally, or who are excluded from your will, are likely to contest the will.

## *DISINHERITANCE*

Disinheritance usually applies to immediate family members (an only child, for example) who would have a claim on your estate if you had no will or if your will were declared invalid. Note that Louisiana is the only state in which you cannot disinherit your children. If you disinherit an immediate family member, it is always wise to state your reasons for doing so in your will. In most other cases, you may effectively disinherit anyone other than your named beneficiaries by simply not including them in your will. If you wish, you may also include a statement in your will specifically omitting all others.

● **Example** ─────────────────────────────────────────────

I hereby specifically exclude from my estate any and all other persons not named previously in this, my Last Will and Testament.

──────────────────────────────────────────────────────────●

*CAUTION:* Completely disinheriting your legal spouse is virtually impossible. In any case, your spouse will be able to take an elective "forced" share of the estate. Remember, disinheriting a close family member can cause controversy in your family. Family members who feel that they have been unfairly disinherited are the source of most will challenges. If you have reason to believe that someone will contest your will, recognize that he or she will probably engage an attorney, and take special care when preparing your will. A properly executed (signed and witnessed) will is very difficult to challenge successfully.

Many of the special situations encountered at different stages of estate planning may be addressed with simple provisions in your will. Evaluating your personal situation and your goals is necessary to determine if additional estate planning measures are needed. If continuing care of dependents, conservation of assets for future generations, or estate taxes are a concern, you should consider a trust or other arrangement. Health and medical expenses are also concerns that can affect estate planning decisions. The Living Will and the Power of Attorney, two common estate planning techniques that address continuing care, conservation of assets, and health concerns, are covered in Chapter 8. The trust is treated in some detail in the next section.

# *Trusts*

A trust is simply defined as giving assets or property to one party (a trustee) to hold, use, or manage for another party (the trust beneficiary). A trust is legally established by the witnessed and notarized execution of a declaration of trust by the creator of the trust (also called the settlor, grantor, trustor, or donor). The trust agreement empowers the trustee to administer the trust and sets out its terms and conditions.

Many techniques of estate planning can be set up with little or no outside help. For example, tax-deductible gifts of up to $10,000 each may be made to children and grandchildren each year by each parent. The preparation of a will; joint titling of real estate and accounts, with a specified right of survivorship; and payment of life insurance policy proceeds to a named beneficiary can all be arranged easily, without ongoing outside assistance being required. A trust, however, requires the services of a trustee, who is empowered to oversee the operation of the trust, in accordance with the guidance contained in the basic trust agreement. Since a trust cannot be effectively used for estate planning purposes without outside assistance, the following material is intended to provide a general overview of trusts so that the type of trust needed can be identified. After review of this material, it is suggested that the components of the trust desired be listed in outline form to provide an informed basis for proceeding with outside assistance. The Trust Checklist on pages 19 and 20 is provided for this purpose.

## PURPOSES OF TRUSTS

Reasons for establishing a trust include:

- Providing for continuing care and education of minor children (or grandchildren).
- Providing income for a surviving spouse.
- Providing for continuing care of a dependent or incompetent adult.
- Providing the assistance and the security of professional management of assets.
- Minimizing federal estate taxes if the combined estate (of husband and wife) will exceed $600,000 upon the death of the surviving spouse.
- Minimizing state inheritance taxes.
- Avoiding the expense, delay, and public record involved in the probate process.

## THE TRUST ENTITY

The establishment of a trust creates a separate legal entity, the trust, which has ownership and/or title of property transferred to it. As a separate legal entity, the trust must be given a Federal Employer Identification Number (FEIN), and separate state and federal income tax returns must be filed if the trust's income exceeds $600 annually. Generally, the trust holds title to all its assets, is managed by a trustee, and is owned by the beneficiary(ies). Functionally, a trust is very similar to a private investment corporation. The trustee should keep accurate accounts and report on the trust's status to the beneficiaries (owners) on a regular basis.

## THE TIMING OF TRUST DISTRIBUTION

The reasons for establishing a trust affect its terms. An arrangement suitable for one stage of family life, addressing care of minor children in the event of the death of one or both parents, becomes functionally obsolete when the children reach adulthood and are presumed capable of managing their own affairs. A trust to pass on family real estate to the next generation may be established whenever circumstances warrant it. Establishing a trust to provide a source of funds for the continuing care of a spouse or relative who has, or may have, medical problems is often a concern in later life. Tax planning reasons for establishing a trust are directly related to the present and anticipated value of your estate.

A trust can be structured to pay all, or a portion of, the trust principal to the trust beneficiary(ies) at various times, either on specific dates, such as birthdays, or over multiyear periods.

Examples of timing trust principal distribution include:

- All of the principal to beneficiary(ies) on January 1, 2000.
- Each beneficiary's principal to be paid in full upon his or her twenty-fifth birthday.
- Beneficiary to receive one-third of the principal 10 years from the date of the trust agreement, one-half of the remaining principal 5 years later, and the balance of the principal 20 years from the date of the trust agreement.

  | 10 years | $\frac{1}{3}$ |
  | 15 years ($\frac{1}{2} \times \frac{2}{3}$) | $\frac{1}{3}$ |
  | 20 years (balance) | $\frac{1}{3}$ |

- All to beneficiaries upon sale of trust assets, per trust agreement.

When the principal balance of the trust is fully paid to the trust beneficiary(ies), the trust is terminated.

Trusts can be established on either a revocable or an irrevocable basis. An irrevocable trust cannot be changed, whereas a revocable trust can be terminated at the trustee's discretion. At present, there are no federal income or estate tax advantages to a revocable trust.

## THE TRUSTEE

Clearly, the person or organization chosen as trustee has a significant bearing on how the trust is structured. If a third-party trustee, either an individual or an organization, is appointed, the trustee should be bonded in the amount of the trust to protect the interests of the beneficiary(ies). Compensation of the trustee for investment, management, disbursement, and state and federal tax filings should be established and agreed on before a trust is set up. Third-party trustee fees vary with the size, term, and complexity of the trust, and it is wise to obtain several quotes. If the trust has a relatively long term, it is also desirable to select an alternate trustee to serve in case the first trustee becomes incapacitated or is otherwise unable to serve.

Trusts can be organized either as "living" trusts (*inter vivos* trusts) or as "testamentary" trusts (established upon death). If you set up a living trust, you can also be the trustee. Generally, a revocable trust is preferable if you plan to act as the trustee or wish to assess the performance of a third-party trustee.

## THE FUNDING OF TRUSTS

Living trusts are funded with wholly owned assets such as cash, stocks, bonds, and real estate. A testamentary trust can be funded with wholly owned assets or life insurance policy proceeds. The initial funding of a trust is its principal. Funds earned from the trust principal, such as interest, dividends, and rents, are considered as trust income. Many trusts are designed to preserve the principal until termination, with the trust income being distributed to the trust beneficiaries in a timely manner for their benefit. In other cases, the trust may be structured to reinvest all income, thereby creating a larger principal balance to be paid out when the trust is terminated.

If the trust is funded with real estate, you may also grant a lifetime-use provision for a spouse or others, particularly if they are not to be beneficiaries of the trust upon its termination. This is accomplished by adding a life estate interest clause to the deed of the property involved before its transfer to the trust. A beneficiary of a trust has vested ownership in all, or part of, the trust principal and income. Unless otherwise specified, ownership of a trust interest is an asset to the owner and, as such, can become a part of the owner's estate.

# *Trust Checklist*

### PURPOSE(S) OF TRUST

_____     Continuing care/income

_____     Maintenance of ownership

_____     Timed distribution of assets

_____     Privacy/avoiding probate

_____     Tax considerations

### TYPE OF TRUST

_____     Testamentary trust

_____     Living trust (*inter vivos*)

### NATURE OF TRUST

_____     Irrevocable

_____     Revocable

### TRUSTEE

_____     Third party

_____     Self/owner(s)

### TRUST ASSET(S)

_____     Real estate

_____     Stocks/bonds

_____     Cash

_____     Income-producing asset(s)

*(continued)*

# *Trust Checklist (continued)*

SOURCE OF TRUST ASSETS

_____     Lifetime transfer(s)

_____     Estate

_____     Life insurance proceeds

TERM OF TRUST

_____     Years

TRUST OWNERS/INCOME BENEFICIARY(IES)

_____

_____

_____

_____

TIMING OF TRUST DISTRIBUTION

Income _____

_____

_____

Principal/Asset(s) _____

_____

_____

Date _____

# CHAPTER *2*

# *Writing Your Will*

*Will: (a) A legal statement of a person's wishes concerning the disposal of his property after death; (b) the document containing this.*

*Webster's New Twentieth Century Dictionary*, 2nd Ed.,
Simon & Schuster, New York, 1983

Any capable adult, by following simple formalities, can prepare and execute a valid will with little difficulty. Because, in most states, the laws regarding wills have their origins in English Common Law, the form and formalities of a testamentary will are clearly established. Although there is no strictly "standard" format, the will forms in this book, as do most wills, contain an opening clause, provisions to name and empower an Executor, a space for bequests, and an attestation clause for signing by witnesses. This chapter discusses the basic form of a testamentary will and key information regarding your Executor and witnesses. Other forms related to your will—self-proving certificates and codicils—are also explained.

## *Forms and Formalities*

Regardless of the content, complexity, and length of your will, it shares common characteristics with all other wills. A testamentary will must contain a statement of intent, be signed by the Testator, and be witnessed by at least two persons (three in Louisiana and Vermont) who are not connected to your estate. The will forms in this book contain an opening clause to identify the Testator and declare intent and an "attestation" clause for signing by witnesses. The forms also contain a section to name and empower your chosen

Executor and, of course, a section reserved for bequests. Most testamentary wills are similar in form, no matter how they are prepared.

The opening clause is included in all testamentary (witnessed) wills to identify the Testator fully, set out the legal jurisdiction of residence, and declare that the document is the last will and testament, revoking all prior wills and codicils. Though not required, most opening clauses include a statement asserting the soundness of mind and memory of the Testator and stating that the will has been prepared free of influence or threat by others.

● **Example** ─────────────────────────────────────────────────

### Last Will and Testament

I, _____Naomi Lee Spencer Light_____, resident of the _____County_____ of _____Botetourt_____ in the State of _____Virginia_____, being of sound mind, do make and declare the following to be my LAST WILL AND TESTAMENT and expressly revoke all my prior wills and codicils and certify that I am not acting under undue influence, duress, or menace.

## Your Executor

The "Executor" section on the will forms provides space to list your chosen Executor and an alternate. Your Executor, usually a beneficiary, will handle the details of settling your estate and fulfill the terms of your will. Naming an alternate Executor can ensure that a person you have chosen administers your estate if your first-named Executor is unable or unwilling to serve.

● **Example** ─────────────────────────────────────────────────

I. EXECUTOR

I appoint _____Paul Samuel Light, my husband_____, EXECUTOR of this my LAST WILL AND TESTAMENT. If this EXECUTOR is unable to serve for any reason, then I appoint _____Carroll Abraham Light, my son_____, EXECUTOR.

You may name, with only a few limitations, any person you choose as the Executor of your estate. In all states, the person chosen must be competent, of legal age, and a U.S. citizen. It is usually practical to have an Executor who lives in the same state; however, it is not a requirement. To save expense and maintain privacy, most people name as their Executor their spouse, a major beneficiary, a family member, or a friend. When complicated or extensive estate administration is required, your choice of Executor becomes more critical. Trust and confidence, as well as cost, are important considerations when you choose your Executor.

Be sure to discuss and confirm your plans with your chosen Executor. A person nominated as Executor can refuse appointment or petition the court to be released from his or her duties after appointment if unable to serve. In such cases, the alternate Executor named in your will is appointed.

## The Role of the Executor

The Executor of an estate is required to:

- Submit the will to the court for probate to establish its validity.
- Inventory all assets of the estate.
- Collect funds due the Testator.
- Pay just debts of the Testator.
- File state and federal tax returns.
- Distribute the estate in accordance with the terms of the will.
- Submit receipts from all beneficiaries and a final accounting of receipts and disbursements to the court.

The Executor will act as your agent to collect and conserve the assets of your estate and pay expenses, debts, and taxes on your behalf. After all liabilities are paid, the Executor distributes the remainder of the estate according to the terms of the will. Any capable, competent adult should have little difficulty in settling a simple estate. After the estate is closed by the court, the duties and powers of the Executor are ended.

You may name Co-Executors to share the duties of administering your estate. Naming a Co-Executor who is unlikely to predecease you or to move away from your community guards against problems created by distance and unpredictability. Frequently, adult children are named as Co-Executors, particularly if the estate is to be divided between them. If extensive or complicated estate administration is needed, you may consider naming a bank, a financial institution, an attorney, or another qualified person as Executor. Bear in mind that your Executor can employ professional assistance and therefore need not perform all the duties of closing the estate alone.

If you've appointed a major beneficiary as Executor, there is usually no reason to compensate that person for performing the duties required to settle your estate. Executor fees are a liability to the estate and therefore reduce the amount available to the beneficiaries. If your Executor feels that the specified compensation is inadequate, he or she may petition the court to award reasonable compensation. "Reasonable" compensation is defined in most states as a percentage (usually 3 to 5 percent) of the value of the estate. Avoiding the expense of court-ordered Executor fees is a good reason to name your major beneficiary as Executor. If you are considering someone other than a beneficiary as Executor, discuss your plans carefully and agree to compensation before making your final selection. Remember, provisions or instructions in a will that keep the estate open for an extended period of time require continuing administration by the Executor.

In order to settle your estate efficiently, your Executor will need certain information about you, your beneficiaries, and the real and personal property you own. The simplest method of providing that information is to discuss your plans fully with your Executor and furnish him or her with the needed information. Your Executor plays a vital role in your estate plan and should be as informed as necessary to act on your behalf. The Record Set in this book includes Executor Data sheets on which to list the basic information your Executor will need.

The Executor of your estate is required by law to pay your debts, funeral expenses, and taxes. Because of the legal requirement that these obligations be met, there is no need to specify their payment in your will. All states grant sufficient powers to allow your Executor to settle your estate.

## ● Example

The EXECUTOR is empowered to carry out all provisions of this WILL.

The EXECUTOR shall have all statutory powers available under state law.

In addition to the nomination of the Executor and alternate and the designation of duties and powers, a clause is frequently included in wills to free the Executor from obtaining a surety bond. A surety bond, equal to the value of the estate, is usually required by law if direction is not included specifically to release the Executor from obtaining a bond. When the Executor you nominate is a person you know and trust, the cost of such a bond is an unnecessary expense to your estate. The first six will forms in the Document Set at the back of this book contain this printed clause.

## ● Example

The EXECUTOR named shall not be required to post surety bond.

Those who wish to guard against the possibility of illegal or irresponsible administration by the Executor may specify that the Executor post a surety bond. Some situations, although few, may call for this measure. The last two sets of will forms do not include a printed statement to release the Executor from bond requirements, although you may write or type one in. If you wish to require a bond of your Executor, you should make a statement to that effect.

● **Example**

I direct that the named Executor post a surety bond equal to the value of my estate.

## NAMING AN OUT-OF-STATE EXECUTOR

All states allow nonresidents to act as Executors, and most states place no restrictions or additional requirements on nonresidents. States with restrictions, however, usually require a nonresident Executor to be a primary beneficiary or close family member. In some states, a nonresident Executor is required to secure a bond or have a state resident act as a personal representative. Those who name a nonresident Executor should have important estate and personal information available to the Executor and discuss any special plans or instructions with him or her. Your Executor will need detailed personal and financial information in order to settle your estate as quickly and inexpensively as possible. Remember, naming someone in a distant state as your Executor will involve additional travel and expense. Whenever possible, it is best to name a resident of your state as your Executor.

# Outside Appraisal of the Estate

An additional clause included in many wills directs that no outside appraisal of the estate be made. An outside appraisal is usually unnecessary unless the estate is substantial, complex, or ordered by the court for estate tax valuation. In most states, one or more appraisals may be required, with the costs being paid from the estate, unless a specific direction such as the following is included.

● **Example**

I direct that no outside appraisal of my estate be made unless required for estate tax purposes.

# Bequests

Because the primary purpose of a will is to dispose of the estate of the Testator, all wills contain bequests. The bequests you make in your will generally fall into two categories: specific bequests and a residuary bequest. Specific bequests are gifts of specifically identified assets or stated amounts of money.

● **Example**

I give my 1936 Ford Sedan, SN 12345765, to my brother, Samuel Gordon Stull.

A residual bequest disposes of all the property not set out in specific bequests. A residuary bequest in a will disposes of personal items and other property not specifically included in other bequests.

● **Example**

I give all the residue of my estate to the American Heart Association, 706 Fifth Avenue, New York, New York, for the general purposes of the organization.

# Witnessing Your Will

A testamentary will must be witnessed according to the statutory requirements of the state in which it is written. The role of witnesses is simple but extremely important. The witnesses attest that you signed and dated your will in their presence and were of sound mind and acting voluntarily when you did so. The witnesses attest to these facts by signing and dating your will as witnesses. If anyone questions the authenticity of your will, the witnesses may be called upon to verify that you signed the document in their presence. For this reason, the witnesses should always list their full names and addresses. The basic procedure to follow when you are ready to sign and date your will is as follows:

1. Choose your witnesses carefully, and be sure to have them available when you are ready to sign and date your will.
2. Sign and date your will in the presence of all your witnesses. (You may orally declare to the witnesses that the document is your last will and testament.)

3. Have each witness sign and date the document in your presence and in the presence of each other. Be sure witnesses list their residential addresses.

Following this simple procedure can help assure that your will is declared valid and quickly admitted for probate. Choosing your witnesses carefully is also an important consideration when preparing your will.

Two witnesses are required in all states except Louisiana and Vermont, which require three. You may have more than the required number of witnesses but never less. Your witnesses must be of legal age, of sound mind, and, in most states, "disinterested." A disinterested witness is a person who has no interest in your estate, either personally or through others. In many states, witnesses and their immediate families are prohibited by law from sharing in the estate of the Testator, whereas other states limit the share of an estate the witnesses may take. In states where persons who have an interest in an estate are disqualified as witnesses, a will can be declared void. Consider your witnesses carefully; coworkers, friends, neighbors, and fellow church members are often good choices. Choosing witnesses who are stable community members, who are in good health, and who have no interest in your estate is always wise.

Your witnesses must be *together* to see you sign and date your will or codicil. Since your witnesses attest that you are not under duress, menace, or undue influence, you may wish to state that, as well as declaring that the document you are signing is your last will and testament (or codicil). The contents may be kept private; there is no need for your witnesses to have any knowledge of the terms or provisions of the document.

## Self-Proving Your Will

When a will is presented to the court, the witnesses may be called to "prove" (verify) their signatures on the document. Most often, a copy of the will or attestation portion is sent to the witnesses, along with an affidavit to sign and return to the court. If your will is contested or questioned by the court, the witnesses will be required to appear or sign an affidavit.

In all but three states (Illinois, Vermont, and West Virginia), self-proving certificates are recognized. A self-proving certificate verifies that the signatures appearing on the will are those of the Testator and witnesses. After being signed by all, the certificate is notarized and attached to the will. A properly completed and notarized self-proving certificate frees your witnesses from appearing when your will is presented to the court. Although there is no requirement that your will be self-proved, it is a step that should be considered. Settling your estate may be delayed if your witnesses move to an unknown address or for some other reason are difficult to locate when needed. To self-prove your will, you and your witnesses must personally appear before a notary public. The notary can complete the self-proving certificate and notarize the document after everyone has signed.

## *Reviewing Your Will*

The purpose of a will is to document clearly the Testator's intent regarding the disposition of the property that constitutes his or her estate. Periodically, review your estate and family situation to ensure that your will meets your needs. When changing personal circumstances make your existing will invalid or obsolete, revising your will is necessary. Whether you are starting with a simple holographic (wholly handwritten) will or a detailed document including many bequests and multiple contingencies, the first step is to note the type of changes that are necessary.

## *Will Revision Checklist*

_____    Legal residence of Testator

_____    Designated Executor and alternate

_____    Executor bond requirements

_____    Direction regarding outside appraisals of estate

_____    Executor compensation

_____    Addition or deletion of beneficiaries

_____    Addition or deletion of bequests

_____    Addition or deletion of charitable bequests

_____    Addition or deletion of designated guardian(s)

_____    Legal adulthood of children and grandchildren

_____    Creation or deletion of a trust

_____    Estate tax considerations

_____    Other personal changes

If only simple changes are needed, your current valid will can be amended by the addition of a codicil. If more extensive modification is required, you should simply rewrite your will. In either case, the testamentary method—a will or codicil that is signed and dated before witnesses—is recommended.

## Codicils

A codicil is simply a document that specifies a change in your current will, and it must reference your current will. A codicil must be executed—signed and dated before witnesses—in the same manner as a will, and should be physically attached to the will it amends. A codicil may be self-proved, in which case it also self-proves the will amended by the codicil.

A codicil can be used to address immediate changes in your estate plans while you formulate a more comprehensive approach. When preparing a codicil, be sure to use full legal names, state relationships, and use specific language to ensure that your intent is clear. A codicil references your current will by your full legal name and the date the will was executed. Never write on, or cross out, sections of your current will. A sample codicil and self-proving certificate are shown in Chapter 5 (Figures 8 and 9).

The witness procedure for a codicil is the same as that for an original will. The most important point in making sure your will is declared valid is to have it properly witnessed. Your witnesses must be legal adults, must have no interest in the estate, and must attest to your capacity and intent by affixing their signatures in one another's presence to the codicil.

## Rewriting Your Will

If you have several changes to make or if your will is not long, you may find it better to rewrite it completely. When you prepare a new will, its first statement includes revocation of all prior wills and codicils. To eliminate any possible confusion, be sure to destroy the original and all copies of your previous will (including any codicils) *after* you have executed your new will.

## Keeping Your Will Safe

Your will should always be kept in a safe, secure location, along with other important documents. Always notify your Executor of the location of your will. You may wish to leave your will, or an unsigned copy, with your Executor. Your

Executor must have the original document to file with the court when needed.

*CAUTION:* In some states, the contents of safe-deposit boxes are sealed upon the death of the boxholder. If you intend to keep your will in a safe-deposit box, be sure to ask your banker about state laws. If the box is sealed, your Executor may not be able to obtain your will quickly when it is needed.

# CHAPTER *3*

# *Your Property*

Your estate consists of all the property that you personally own. Property consisting of land and any improvements to it is categorized as real property and everything else is designated as personal property. Personal property is further classified as tangible and intangible. Tangible personal property consists of actual items—everything from automobiles and antiques to shoes and socks. Intangible personal property, such as cash, stocks, bonds, and trust share ownership, is representative of value. Intellectual personal property is a form of intangible property and includes copyrights, patents, licenses, and residual performance rights. Both tangible and intangible property may be transferred in your will through individual bequests or as a part of the total estate. In many situations, other estate planning techniques to transfer property, such as joint titling (with right of survivorship), tax-exempt lifetime gifts, or trusts, are more appropriate. Real and personal property, methods of transfer, and related estate planning concerns are discussed in this chapter.

## *Tangible Personal Property*

Your tangible personal property has two components of value, its base cash value and the value of its association with you. Items of one's personal property with little cash value are often treasured by one's loved ones for the positive memories they evoke. Another characteristic of tangible personal property is that its replacement cost generally exceeds its resale value, particularly under forced sale conditions. Almost everyone is aware of the types of bargains available at estate auctions. Recognizing these factors as you review your personal property may prompt additional specific bequests in your will. For example, you may decide that it would be better to give a recently purchased washer and drier, television set, or personal computer to a niece or nephew living nearby rather than to have the items sold and the cash proceeds divided. You also may decide to give keepsake items to those you wish to have them now, when you can personally provide background about their origins and are able to enjoy the giving of the gift. Gifts of tangible personal property made in your will should be specifically identified.

● **Example** ───────────────────────────────────

I give my entire collection of U.S. silver dollars, which are kept in my First National Bank of Richmond, Virginia, safe-deposit box number 231, to my beloved son, Carl Graham White.

Tangible property includes titled personal property, such as cars, trucks, recreational vehicles, boats, and airplanes. Gifts of such property in your will should be identified by description and title, serial, or ID number. You may consider expediting transfer of such personal property by placing it in joint title (with right of survivorship) with your chosen beneficiary. This approach bypasses the probate procedure and may be advantageous for valuable personal property, such as classic automobiles, yachts, and airplanes. Bear in mind that joint titling will require the co-owner's consent if you choose later to sell or exchange the asset involved. Another aspect to consider when reviewing titled personal property is its lien status and how any outstanding balance would be satisfied. If the asset is jointly titled, any liens would become the responsibility of the cotitleholder.

## Intangible Personal Property

Generally, cash, stocks, bonds, and other financial instruments are considered liquid assets. Liquidity simply refers to the speed with which the value of an asset can be converted into currency without loss. Cash, checking, savings, and money market accounts are highly liquid assets and are often designated to fund monetary bequests. Stocks, bonds, and other financial instruments are readily convertible to cash, although the timing of the conversion is often critical to receiving maximum benefit. Transfer of intangible personal property by arrangements that avoid probate, such as joint titling of accounts or assets with beneficiaries, should be considered as part of your estate plan.

## MONETARY GIFTS

When you make monetary bequests in your will, they are deducted from the general assets of your estate after all expenses are paid. If the liquid assets of your estate are insufficient to meet monetary bequests, the Executor may have to sell other real and personal property to fund them. Clearly, the liquidity of your assets is a major consideration when you make specific monetary gifts.

● **Example**

I give my brother, Abraham Lee Light, the sum of $1,000.00.

A gift that is to be paid from a specific source will be paid with funds from the designated source. If the funds from that source are insufficient, and if adequate assets exist in your general estate, the balance may be paid from the general assets. To ensure that your monetary bequests are not reduced or voided, verify that sufficient cash resources are (or will be) available.

● **Example**

I give my sister, Naomi Karen White, the sum of $1,000.00 to be paid from my savings account, #543210, at the 1st National Bank, 101 3rd Street, Salem, Virginia.

If you desire a monetary bequest be used for a specific purpose, be sure to designate the purpose in your bequest.

● **Example**

I give my church, 1st Methodist, 110 Front Street, Richmond, Virginia, the sum of $1,000.00, for the building fund.

Certificates of deposit (CDs), individual retirement accounts (IRAs), and U.S. government savings bonds are somewhat less liquid, since usually they cannot be accessed without penalty (foregone interest and fees) before a specific date. Publicly traded corporate stocks and government and corporate bonds can be highly liquid; however, market fluctuations may make forced sale disadvantageous at certain times. Stock in privately held corporations, limited and regular partnership shares, and private notes are generally the most illiquid forms of commonly held intangible personal property. It is often more beneficial to give intangible personal property directly to your beneficiaries rather than to have it sold to fund monetary bequests.

## ● Example

I give to each of my beloved daughters, Naomi Karen White and Louise Beatrice Hale, 357 shares of my American Telephone and Telegraph (AT&T) preferred stock.

This approach allows the beneficiary to determine the best time to convert the asset into cash. If the beneficiary retains such property for some time, both dividends and fundamental value appreciation may be realized. Often, stock dividends are directed into automatic reinvestments in additional shares. In such a situation, the number of shares and fractional units will be periodically increasing. You may wish your beneficiary to receive the entire amount of stock to prevent the incremental additions from becoming part of your general or residual estate. If this is the case, say so.

## ● Example

I give my grandson, Carroll Abraham Light, II, all of my shares of American Telephone and Telegraph (AT&T) preferred stock.

Bequests of intangible personal property can be for a specific amount, or the assets themselves may be given. For example, you may wish to give the sum of $3000 to each of your grandchildren, or you may prefer to give each a tax-exempt bond or a certain number of shares of a particular stock. If you choose to make monetary bequests, be sure that you specify how the balance of your intangible personal property is to be distributed. This can be done by leaving your entire estate to one or more primary beneficiary(ies) or a trust, except for the specific monetary bequests. Another option is to make your various bequests and end your will with a residual bequest distributing the remainder to a beneficiary you choose. Since intangible personal property generally increases in value over time as interest and/or dividend payments are received, it is important to arrange for distribution of the entire amount.

## *INTELLECTUAL PROPERTY*

Intellectual property, such as copyrights and patents, can be given to a beneficiary in your will. Intellectual property rights typically have long terms and can be renewed. Fees paid for use of intellectual property are royalties and may constitute a valuable portion of your estate. Intellectual property may be held with another, unrelated person, in which case you may transfer only your own interest to your beneficiaries.

● **Example**

I give my wife, Karen Louise Light, my one-half share of patent rights and resultant royalties from the fiberoptic switching system developed with my business associate, Norman James Teller, identified by U.S. Patents G-100689 and G-103746.

It is advisable to refer to the patent or copyright identification number when transferring intellectual property rights. Similarly, if you receive residual payments for television rebroadcast rights, these rights should be clearly identified and given to your chosen beneficiary. Since the value of intellectual property rights is directly related to their use, you should consider leaving special instructions regarding how to maximize their value.

# *Real Property*

Real property consists of land (real estate) and any improvements to or on that land. Real property is characterized by its use. Types of real property include:

### *Unimproved Property*

- Forest.
- Range.
- Marsh.
- Vacant lot.

### *Residential Property*

- Primary residence.
- Second home.
- Lot and mobile home.
- Cooperative apartment.
- Condominium.
- Time-share unit.

### *Income-Producing Property*

- Residential.
- Farm.
- Subdivision.
- Campground.
- Commercial.
    Retail.
    Office.
    Warehouse.
- Industrial.
- Hotel/motel.
- Marina.

The value of each parcel of real property is affected by its location, condition, size, quality, and appropriateness for use. Generally, real property is an appreciating asset, increasing in value over time. Most real property is purchased through a mortgage secured by the property. As the outstanding mortgage balance decreases over time while the total value of the property usually increases, substantial net equity is gained. Often this equity appreciation in real property value constitutes a significant portion of personal net worth.

When making gifts of real property in your will, be sure to identify specifically the real estate involved. This can be achieved by reference to the street address, including the city and state where the property is located. In cases involving a rural route address or unimproved real estate, it is advisable to identify the subject property by the tax number or lot/tract number. This information, which constitutes a brief legal description of the property, is found in the deed and on property tax bills. Clarity is particularly important when identifying real property owned in a state other than your state of residence.

## ● Example

I give my summer home located on Lake Norman, in Mecklenburg County in the state of North Carolina (Tax Map 106, Section 12, Lots 3, 4, and 5), to my daughter, Dawn Lee Hale.

## *DEED OPTIONS*

State property laws govern the forms of real estate ownership and deed options available. In many situations, deed options are used to direct the transfer of real property outside the probate process. Titling property so that it automatically transfers to the beneficiary is a common estate planning technique. It is advisable to review real estate deeds to verify the portion and terms of your current ownership interest.

If you are married and live in a community-property state, all property acquired during the marriage is owned by each spouse in equal shares. Property acquired before or outside the marriage, such as an inheritance, is separate property and is owned individually. Community-property interests, if no other provisions are made, must be disposed of in your will.

***JOINT TITLING / TENANCY BY THE ENTIRETY.*** Joint titling, with right of survivorship, is an option that allows property to transfer without the expense and delay of probate. You may jointly title real property with your spouse or other beneficiary in most states. Tenancy by the entirety, a form of ownership available in some states only to married couples, also transfers property interests to the surviving spouse. The stability of the marriage or of your relationship to the beneficiary should be weighed carefully when planning to title property as joint owners or tenants by the entirety.

If you've titled property so that it transfers automatically, you should also plan for transfer of your estate in the event that you and your spouse or beneficiary die in a common accident or disaster. In such a circumstance, your wills, naming an alternate beneficiary for your estates, can dispose of the jointly held property. Because of the possibility of simultaneous death, your will and that of your spouse or other joint owner should agree on alternate beneficiaries. You and your beneficiaries should have a current will at all times to meet this contingency.

***LIFE ESTATE.*** Another deed option is the creation of a life estate interest in the property on behalf of a person you choose. A life estate is the right to use the property for the holder's lifetime, separate from ownership, which is listed in the name of another, and is a recorded liability against the property. A life estate is established by amending the property deed.

***FACTORS TO CONSIDER.*** When planning the transfer of ownership of residential real estate, many factors should be considered. Will your intended beneficiary live in the property? How will any outstanding mortgage balances be paid? Has the property been in your family for a long time? How will maintenance be dealt with? Clearly, the answer to these and similar concerns can change over time. Plans that your spouse and dependent children occupy your large home usually change after your children settle in their own homes. On the other hand, you may have a second residence or vacation home that your family can enjoy for years.

The same considerations apply to condominium and time-share interests in real property. If you have any outstanding mortgage or lien balances secured by the real estate, including home equity lines of credit, further decisions are needed. Should the mortgage(s) and lien(s) be paid off and the property transferred without any encumbrances? Or do you prefer your beneficiary to receive the equity interest and pay the outstanding balance(s) on the existing terms? You must specify your intent and direct your Executor accordingly in your will. Otherwise, the real property may have to be sold to pay outstanding balances, and your beneficiary would realize only the net after sale, quite possibly under distress conditions yielding less than full value.

## INCOME-PRODUCING PROPERTY

Income-producing property should be reviewed in terms of the amount of active involvement required to maintain the income stream. Simple receipt of interest and/or dividends is essentially a passive function that automatically follows the ownership of account, stock, and bond assets. In contrast, ownership of rental property, a farm, or a private business usually requires informed and active management. If your primary beneficiary is not fully involved in, or willing and able to manage, these operations, the income stream may well be diminished or stop altogether.

If you have commercial or rental property that you currently manage, it may be advisable to make separate arrangements for continuing management. Such arrangements are usually contained in a separate document and referenced in your will.

● **Example** ─────────────────────────────────

I give my apartment building located at 704–709 Laburnham Avenue in the city of Richmond, Virginia (Tax Number 408-10886), to my son, Charles James Hale, and direct my Executor to give my son, Charles James Hale, my instructions regarding property management contained in a letter of instructions dated June 10, 1989.

─────────────────────────────────●

When assessing income-producing property that requires active management, you should consider whether it would be better to have the assets sold and the proceeds distributed to your beneficiaries. In such sales, receiving a fair price in your absence may not be possible without adequate preparation. The type of preparation needed will vary depending on the nature of the property or business and the capability of your associates.

For example, if you own commercial real estate that you actively manage, you may need only to locate a suitable agent or firm that can manage the property, with the ownership and income stream passing to your beneficiaries. As the current owner/manager, you are best qualified to select an agent, based on your own local knowledge. You should discuss your intentions with your prospective agent and obtain a binding agreement fixing the agent's terms of compensation. This agreement should be immediately available to your Executor, with careful guidance set forth in your letter of instructions. You may further provide suggestions as to property value and indicate a strategy to sell your property over a period of years, based on market value and tax considerations. Income-producing property may involve a basic break-even income/expense position while awaiting future sale at appreciated value. In such situations, purchase of additional life insurance to provide for payment of obligations can minimize the risk of loss.

Business and farm operations usually require special arrangements for continuing management. If you actively manage a farm or closely held business, finding a suitable replacement manager is apt to be difficult. If a member of your family has the desire to continue operating the business or farm, that person should be brought into the daily operations as soon as is practicable. If, on the other hand, none of your beneficiaries has the desire or ability to maintain operations, other arrangements will be required. Buy-sell agreements and installment sales are practical options for such transfers.

## Life Insurance

At some stages, review of your net property position may show a shortfall of asset value relative to total liens and liabilities. This can happen even when you have substantial net worth if your primary assets consist of real property or a private business concern. Potential cash shortfall can be covered by life insurance policies to prevent forced sale of real estate and business assets (often at a deep discount). Life insurance can be viewed as contingent intangible personal property. Life insurance policies have owners and name beneficiaries, and their proceeds do not pass through the probate process unless they are payable to the estate of the decedent or to the Executor. Mortgage balance insurance and credit card balance insurance are examples of life insurance that is paid on behalf of the estate and passes through probate. A life insurance policy on the life of another person is considered the property of the policy owner and is valued at the replacement value of the policy.

After making an inventory of your personal property, both tangible and intangible, and identifying your liens and liabilities, you should easily be able to figure your net position. A series of property inventory sheets is included in the Record Set for this purpose.

# CHAPTER 4

# Bequests and Special Instructions

The primary purpose of your will is to set out plans and instructions for your estate. As the sample will in the Introduction illustrates, a will can be very short and direct. Your will can also be a creative document, outlining plans for individual items of your estate, and you may, if you wish, include terms of endearment. The number and type of instructions and bequests in your will should be decided carefully. Before you begin the actual process of writing a will, make a list of beneficiaries and bequests, with correct names and adequate descriptions of gifts. Documents or other records to be listed in your will should be noted by date or reference number. Your chosen Executor and others who have key roles in your plans should be informed and agree to appointment. Other preparation needed to write a will depends on your personal situation and goals. The "execution" of your will requires at least two witnesses (three in Louisiana and Vermont) to see you actually sign and date the document. If you wish to self-prove your will, you and your witnesses must appear before a notary public. Make any necessary arrangements for witnesses or self-proving in advance.

A variety of bequests and special instructions that may be made regarding the disposition of property are illustrated in this chapter. Plan carefully and review your estate, beneficiaries, and goals before beginning to write your bequests.

## Language in Your Will

The language you use when writing bequests or other provisions is critical to establishing intent and can affect the way your estate is distributed. When writing your will, you should always use direct, easily understandable language. Words that do not specifically indicate your intentions can cause confusion when your will is probated. Words such as "wish," "want," "hope," and "believe" only suggest your intentions rather than stating them, and therefore may not be legally binding, as in the following statement.

### ● Unclear Intent

I *wish* my nephew, Charles James Hale, to have my 1939 Chevrolet, SN 12345.

Although this statement may indicate that it is your *desire* that your nephew have the car, there is no clear statement of your *intent* that he have it. A clear statement follows.

### ● Clear Intent

I *give* my 1939 Chevrolet, SN 12345, to my nephew, Charles James Hale.

The use of simple, direct language helps ensure that your estate plan is followed. There is no requirement that you use legal terms or phrases or fancy words; just be sure that your intent is obvious by stating it clearly and simply. Including terms of endearment or explanation when writing your bequests is a matter of personal choice. Stating your relationship to the beneficiary in the bequest helps make the identity obvious and avoids confusion.

Do not use the term "heir(s)" in your will. In law, an heir is any person who might be entitled to a portion of your estate if you were to die intestate, that is, without a valid will. The rules of intestate succession vary from state to state and, hence, so do possible heirs. The term "beneficiary" is appropriate when referring to those whom you wish to receive a portion of your estate under your will.

If you have a previous will, it may contain legal terms or phrases that are unfamiliar to you. Keep in mind that a will can convey your wishes only if you completely understand its contents. Two common phrases found in wills are "*per stirpes*" and "*per capita,*" both of which refer to methods of distribution.

"*Per stirpes*" (literally, "by the root") means distribution to descendants. Be aware that *per stirpes* distribution applies to your *direct* descendants only, that is, children, grandchildren, and great-grandchildren. A bequest to one of your children made *per stirpes* would be distributed to that child's children if your child is not alive when your will is probated. If that child had no surviving children (issue), the share would be distributed equally among your other descendants.

● **Example**

I give my farmland in Botetourt County, Virginia, Parcels 104-1178, 101-4712, and 104-118, to my three beloved children, Abraham Lee Light, Naomi Karen White, and Louise Beatrice Hale, in equal shares, per stirpes.

"*Per capita*" ("by heads") means equal distribution to those named. In *per capita* distribution, only those named who are living at the time the will is presented for probate will share equally. If you direct that your estate be distributed to your children on a *per capita* basis, and one of your children named does not survive you, their descendants (if any) would receive nothing, and their share would be equally distributed to the other named beneficiaries. If, however, you direct that your estate be distributed *per capita* to "issue" surviving you, then your estate would be divided equally among all your living descendants, children, grandchildren, and great-grandchildren.

When writing your will, choose your words carefully so that your intent is clear. Specific identification of people and property and direct phrasing of instructions are the keys to clarity. Your will should be written so that it is simple to understand and not subject to misinterpretation. Keeping your will current also helps to make it simple and clear.

## Evaluating Your Estate

As discussed in Chapter 3, preparing a will usually begins with making an inventory of the property and assets of your estate. A careful review of real and personal property can reveal assets that have special significance and value to you and your beneficiaries. Real property that has been passed from generation to generation can have value to family members far beyond its monetary worth. The history and memories associated with land and homes often provide a family with a sense of unity, linking past, present, and future generations. Continuity of family ownership of such property can be important when you choose your beneficiaries.

Family history is often tied to items of personal property as well. Jewelry, antiques, household items, and other personal property can have a history of ownership spanning several generations. Although often overlooked, gifts of personal items can be of immense value to the beneficiaries who receive them. Carefully review the origins and significance of all personal property when making an inventory. A description of the item and its place in the history of your family can make it a treasure of great worth to the beneficiary.

After making an inventory of the property you intend to give, you must decide who will receive the gift. The health, age, and location of your beneficiaries may affect the way you write your will. If, for instance, a beneficiary is unable to drive, a gift of a car will have little value. You may ask your intended beneficiaries if certain personal or household items would be of special value or interest to them. Carefully consider situations that may involve a division of property between beneficiaries. Disagreements may be prevented by detailing, either by prior discussion or in your will, the manner in which property should be divided. If beneficiaries live in distant locations, the cost of transporting items such as large household goods may be prohibitive.

Note your plans for beneficiaries who are minors or not mature enough to be entrusted with a gift of either cash or other personal property. The safekeeping of such gifts may be entrusted to a relative or, in the case of cash, distributed through other methods, such as a trust. Decisions regarding charitable bequests should include the amount of the gift and the purpose for which it is to be used. The full names and addresses of beneficiaries, along with descriptions of gifts, can be especially useful to your Executor in the probate process.

## *Identifying Beneficiaries and Bequests*

When making gifts of personal property, it is very important to identify fully the gift and the beneficiary. Without adequate identification, confusion may result when your will is probated.

● **Unclear**

I give my ring to my nephew, Charles.

Which ring? How many nephews named Charles are there? You can easily avoid problems of this type by carefully identifying the gift and the beneficiary.

● **Clear**

I give my gold Masonic ring, inscribed A.L.L., to my nephew, Charles James Hale.

Obviously, the more bequests and beneficiaries you have, the more important identification becomes. Never rely on a single name or a vague description to identify your beneficiaries or bequests.

● **Unclear**

I give my entire estate to my cousins in equal shares.

Such a statement may result in the probate court defining the term "cousin" to mean all the people who fall within a strict legal interpretation of that term. First cousins, second cousins, third cousins, cousins you did not realize you had!

● **Unclear**

I give my entire estate to my children, in equal shares.

Similarly, the preceding statement means *all* your children, by previous marriage(s), illegitimate, and otherwise. Be very careful to name each beneficiary. Never describe a beneficiary or a group of beneficiaries in general terms.

## Bequests

Generally, there are no limitations on your ability to leave your estate to whomever you desire. Exceptions to this right to dispose of your property may apply if you are married. Some states grant a "dower" or "curtesy" right to a surviving spouse. Such a right determines a minimum amount of an estate the surviving spouse is entitled to. Louisiana, in addition to maintaining spousal rights, requires that a Testator not totally disinherit his or her children.

Another restriction on your freedom to dispose of your estate as you wish applies to conditional bequests. Conditional bequests that require a beneficiary to act in an unreasonable manner or to do something irrational or illegal to receive his or her bequest should be avoided. If a condition is illegal or against public policy, the court may choose to ignore it and grant the bequest. If a beneficiary objects to the condition, he or she may simply refuse the bequest. The condition, and the method of determining when and if it is satisfied, must be set out. Conditional bequests usually result in your estate's being kept open until the conditions are met and may require extensive time and effort on the part of your Executor. If controlling the actions of your beneficiaries is a vital concern, you should consider a trust or other arrangement.

If you make a bequest of personal property such as a specific automobile, and later sell or dispose of the car, it will obviously not be a part of your final estate. Property that no longer exists in your estate when your will is probated is "adeemed," and therefore the beneficiary cannot receive it. When ademption occurs, that particular bequest fails, although the other terms of the will are not affected.

If you leave monetary gifts in excess of the assets of your estate, those gifts may be "abated." This simply means that each beneficiary's share is reduced proportionally.

● **Example**

I give my sons, Samuel Gordon Stull and Paul Leslie Stull, the sum of $100,000.00 each.

If, after all debts, taxes, and funeral expenses are settled, only $150,000 remained of the Testator's estate, each son would receive $75,000.

## CONTINGENT BEQUESTS

At many times in life, a single beneficiary is named to receive the entire estate of the Testator.

● **Example**

I give my entire estate to my beloved wife, Naomi Lee Spencer Light.

This simple bequest is direct, easy to understand, and fully identifies the beneficiary. The "entire estate" includes *all* the real and personal property owned by the Testator at the time of death. A person who receives the entire estate of the Testator is known as the "sole beneficiary." Although this bequest is complete, it makes no provisions for the distribution of the estate if the sole beneficiary were to die at the same time or soon after the Testator. Naming a contingent beneficiary to receive the bequest, in case the Testator and primary beneficiary die at the same time, is extremely important.

● **Example**

I give my entire estate to my wife, Karen Louise Greene Light, if she survives me by 180 days. If she does not survive me by 180 days, then I give my entire estate to my son, Abraham Lee Light.

In this bequest, the Testator has clearly stated that his spouse must survive him by six months in order to receive that bequest. This can prevent the estate from being transferred prematurely and can provide tax advantages if the estate is substantial.

Many times, bequests are made contingent on the beneficiary outliving the testator by a specified amount of time.

● **Example**

I give my son, Abraham Lee Light, my Parker shotgun, SN 456789, if he survives me by 180 days.

If the son died less than six months after the Testator, the bequest would fail, and the property would revert to the general estate. Many states require by law that beneficiaries named in a will survive the Testator by a minimum length of time (ranging from 5 to 30 days). A beneficiary who does not live the amount of time specified by law or in the will is considered to have predeceased the Testator, and the bequest is not distributed but remains a part of the general or residual estate.

You may also name a contingent, or alternate, beneficiary to receive the gift when you make a bequest.

● **Example**

I give my sister, Louise Beatrice Hale, my diamond dinner ring, inscribed N.K.L. If she does not survive me, then I give the ring to my niece, Dawn Lee Hale.

In this situation, the sister will receive the ring if she survives the Testator; if not, the niece will be the beneficiary. By naming an alternate beneficiary, you can be sure that someone you choose will receive a specific item or asset.

It is especially important for married people to designate an alternate beneficiary.

● **Example**

I give all my estate to my wife, Rachel Beatrice Stull. If she does not survive me by 180 days, then I give my estate, in equal shares, to my cousin, Gordon Leslie Stull, and the Pennsylvania Baptist Children's Home, Inc., Hershey, Pennsylvania.

In the preceding example, if the Testator and his spouse were to die in a common accident, there would be no question of his intent that the estate be divided equally between his alternate beneficiaries.

Care taken in planning your bequests can ensure that your estate is distributed to the beneficiaries you choose.

## RESIDUAL BEQUESTS

Anything left of your estate after your property is distributed by the terms of your will is known as the residue of your estate. If you have directed the disposition of *all* your property, there will be no residue.

● **Example**

I give my *entire* estate to my sons, Samuel Gordon Stull and Paul Leslie Stull, in equal shares.

In this example, the will disposes of the entire estate of the Testator. Therefore, no residue remains in the estate.

If you've disposed of your entire estate in your will, there is no need for a residual bequest. Those who have disposed of their estate by individual bequests may have a residual estate. A bequest of property that is not distributed becomes part of your residual estate.

● **Example**

I give my sons, Samuel Gordon Stull and Paul Leslie Stull, the sum of $50,000.00 each.

Suppose that after all expenses are paid and the $50,000 bequests are fulfilled, $10,000 remains in the Testator's estate. A residual bequest allows the Testator to provide for anything left of the estate.

● **Example**

I give my sons, Samuel Gordon Stull and Paul Leslie Stull, the sum of $50,000.00 each. I give all the residue of my estate to the American Cancer Society, 101 First Street, Los Angeles, California.

If you intend to make a residual bequest, be sure to consider your situation carefully, since the actual amount of the residue of your estate may be more than you planned. If there is no residual estate, then the residual bequest will have no effect. Conversely, the residual estate could become significantly larger than anticipated. In the preceding example, if the Testator had bought an airline ticket with a credit card that automatically issued life insurance and if the plane crashed, killing the Testator, the residue of his estate would be increased by the amount of the life insurance issued. Assuming that the policy paid out $200,000 to the estate, the residue would change from $10,000 to $210,000, all of which would go to the charity named. Clearly, the Testator had not actually intended the charity to receive more than his sons; yet this is what would happen.

## CHARITABLE BEQUESTS

The same care and thought given to other gifts should be applied to charitable bequests. It's particularly important to identify the charity or organization by full name and address, as many charities, churches, and organizations have similar names.

● **Example**

I give the sum of $500.00 to the American Heart Foundation, located at 415 Melrose Avenue, Los Angeles, California.

The purpose of your charitable bequest may also be designated.

● **Example**

I give Brooklyn College, Brooklyn, New York, the sum of $500.00, for the library fund.

Many colleges and charitable institutions provide assistance for those who wish to make a gift. If you are considering a substantial bequest, discuss the gift with a representative of the beneficiary organization. Such organizations often employ estate planning personnel to assist contributors with tax-advantageous methods of giving. Charitable bequests, like all other provisions included in your will, should be reviewed periodically for accuracy and applicability.

## Special Instructions

Provisions and instructions are included in a will to address the personal needs and goals of the Testator. You may include any legal, reasonable instructions regarding the disposition of your estate in your will. Keep in mind that the probate court cannot add to, or delete from, the instructions you have made concerning your estate. For this reason, it is always wise to make any instructions direct, complete, and to the point. Be sure to consider fully the intended result of any instructions to be sure that they will have the effect you desire. Never include an unneeded or irrelevant instruction that could be misinterpreted and could conflict with other terms of your will. The same cautions that apply when wording bequests apply to instructions in your will. Avoid the use of vague or contradictory terms, and be sure your intentions are stated clearly.

● **Example**

I direct my Executor to arrange that I be buried in the Light family cemetery located near the community of Fincastle, Virginia, on Rural Route 625-E.

This provision is clear in its purpose and language. The Testator has directed the Executor to arrange burial in the family cemetery; the description is adequate, and the intent is plain. The directions of the Testator would be followed, assuming that the will was readily available and that the Executor acted quickly. Provisions included in your will that are time-sensitive, such as burial instructions, may not be followed if your will is not immediately available to your Executor or alternate. When including provisions of this type, be sure to inform your Executor of your plans.

A provision in your will may be set out to specify the length of time beneficiaries must survive you in order to receive bequests.

● **Example**

If any beneficiary named in this, my last will, does not survive me by 180 days, then that beneficiary shall be deemed to have predeceased me.

Any beneficiary named in this will must survive the Testator by the length of time stated before the bequest is distributed. The purpose of setting out a provision such as this is to ensure that a gift won't be made to a person who dies very soon after the Testator and therefore would get no real benefit from, or use of, the bequest. The gift would revert to the estate of the Testator and therefore be available to be distributed by the Testator's will. If no provision were made, and the beneficiary died suddenly after the Testator, the bequest would become a part of the estate of the beneficiary. You may state the time a beneficiary must survive you in each bequest or make a stipulation regarding all beneficiaries in a single provision.

Provisions can be used to set out your plans for resolving any disagreements that may arise over the way your estate is divided.

● **Example**

I direct my Executor to fairly settle any disagreement that may arise over the division of my furniture and household goods, which I have left in equal shares to my son, Abraham Lee Light, and my daughter, Naomi Karen Light.

The Executor is clearly instructed to settle any controversy that may occur regarding the division of the Testator's furniture or other household goods. Rather than directing, and listing, every item individually, the Testator has given this bequest in equal shares and named the Executor to settle any disagreements.

Special instructions are often included in a will to provide for the welfare and disposition of pets.

● **Example**

I direct my Executor to find caring homes for my two dogs, Bruno and Otis. Any reasonable expenses incurred while finding new homes for them is to be paid from my estate.

The Executor of this estate is directed to find homes for the two dogs and is authorized to incur reasonable expenses for boarding, food, and other costs. This example illustrates the detail you may include when writing special instructions or provisions.

You may set out compensation for your Executor in your will.

● **Example**

I give my Executor, Thomas Lee Smith, the sum of $2,000.00 in appreciation of his efforts on my behalf in settling my estate.

Remember, there is usually no reason to compensate an Executor who is a primary beneficiary beyond the gifts made in your will. To do so means that your Executor's (beneficiary's) share of the estate, like that of other beneficiaries, will be reduced by the amount specified for the Executor. Your Executor will have to report any compensation as personal income. Also, be aware that all states set out an amount—usually expressed as a percent (3 to 5 percent) of the value of the estate—as reasonable compensation that an Executor may claim for acting on your behalf. If you have named an Executor who is not a beneficiary and have specified as compensation an amount that is substantially less than the courts deem appropriate, the Executor may petition the court for the higher amount allowed by law.

Your will may include a provision stating that if any beneficiary of your will should contest the will, that beneficiary is to receive nothing. This "no contest" provision is known as an *in terrorem* clause. If an *in terrorem* clause relates to a conditional bequest, it may not be accepted by the probate court. Usually, an *in terrorem* clause is included to reinforce the intent of the Testator who has reason to anticipate a challenge to the will.

# CHAPTER 5

# A Family and Its Estate: A Story with Sample Documents

This story of the fictitious Light family traces the growth of the Light family estate from the beginning of the 20th century. Completed wills and related documents appear at the end of the story to illustrate how this family transferred its property from generation to generation.

*NOTE:* The signature and witness block has been omitted from the sample wills in this chapter to save space. All testamentary wills must be signed and witnessed according to state requirements.

## The Light Family at the Turn of the Century

Brandy Run Farm was established in Botetourt County, Virginia, by Paul Samuel Light in 1896. Paul Samuel Light's will, which was probated after his death in 1933, appears in the Introduction.

Paul's son, Carroll Abraham Light, first opened his eyes to the 20th century at Brandy Run Farm on January 2, 1900. He and his family would be touched by three wars in the next 90 years.

# Remembering

In 1988, Abraham Lee Light, Carroll's son, was called on to settle his mother's estate. He was 53 years old. He and his aunt, Mary Alice Light, were now the senior members of the Light family. Brandy Run, the family farm, established before the turn of the century by his grandfather, Paul Samuel Light, was prosperous. His father, Carroll Abraham Light, and Mary Alice had both been born there. In time, Mary Alice would see her last mountain sunset from the old south porch. His own grandchildren were just discovering the fun of playing next to the small stream, Brandy Run. He felt the continuity and stability his family took from the land.

## 1900–1920

### Light Family Key Dates

| Date | Name | Event | Location |
|------|------|-------|----------|
| 1900 | Carroll Abraham Light | Born | Brandy Run Farm, Virginia |
| 1907 | Nathaniel Benjamin Greene Louise Karen Connor | Married | New York, New York |
| 1908 | Rachel Beatrice Greene | Born | Tarrytown, New York |
| 1909 | Louise Connor Greene | Born | Tarrytown, New York |
| 1910 | Mary Alice Light | Born | Brandy Run Farm, Virginia |
| 1912 | Karen Louise Greene | Born | Tarrytown, New York |
| *1918 | Carroll Abraham Light | World War I | France |

*Will sample related to event shown.

Abraham looked through the file of family documents he had assembled from his mother's papers. The simple holographic will his father had written in 1918, leaving everything to his sister, Mary Alice, prior to shipping out to France in the last days of World War I, impressed him with its maturity. (See Figure 3.)

*Being of sound mind, I hereby write my Last Will and Testament. I give my entire estate to my dear sister, Mary Alice Light, and appoint my father, Paul Samuel Light, as my Executor.*

*Carroll Abraham Light*
*May 13, 1918*
*Norfolk, Virginia*

Figure 3

## 1920–1940

### Light Family Key Dates

| Date | Name | Event | Location |
|------|------|-------|----------|
| 1920 | Carroll Abraham Light | | |
| | June Susan Eaton | Married | Bedford County, Virginia |
| 1921 | Samuel Paul Light | Born | Bedford County, Virginia |
| 1927 | June Susan Eaton | Leaves | Texas |
| 1928 | Carroll Abraham Light | Divorced | Bedford County, Virginia |
| 1929 | Louise Connor Greene | | |
| | George Walter Larson | Married | Tarrytown, New York |
| 1929 | Susan Elizabeth Larson | Born | Tarrytown, New York |
| 1930 | Rachel Beatrice Greene | | |
| | Samuel Grice Stull | Married | Tarrytown, New York |
| 1930 | Karen Louise Greene | College | Hollins, Virginia |
| 1932 | Charlene Ruth Larson | Born | Tarrytown, New York |
| *1933 | Paul Samuel Light | Died | Brandy Run Farm, Virginia |
| 1934 | Carroll Abraham Light | | |
| | Karen Louise Greene | Married | Tarrytown, New York |
| 1936 | Abraham Lee Light | Born | Alhambra, California |
| 1939 | Naomi Karen Light | Born | Alhambra, California |

*Will sample related to event shown in Introduction.

After his return from Europe, Carroll Light married June Susan Eaton of Bedford County, Virginia; in 1921, they had a son, Samuel Paul Light. Six years later, June deserted Carroll and Samuel and moved to Texas. Subsequently, Carroll enrolled in college, taking engineering courses. His parents helped with young Sam.

Carroll divorced June and, four years later, met Karen Louise Greene, who was then starting her junior year at Hollins College, majoring in English. Karen was from Tarrytown, New York, and was the youngest of the three daughters of Nathaniel Benjamin Greene and his wife, the former Louise Karen Connor. Karen's father, Nathaniel, had taken over his father's clothing manufacturing business in Brooklyn, and the family lived well.

Louise Connor Greene ("Connie") was the first of the Greene sisters to marry. She wed George Walter Larson, a jazz musician, in February 1929. In September of 1929, Karen's niece, Susan Elizabeth Larson, was born. The following year, Karen's other sister, Rachel, married Samuel Grice Stull, a banker from Philadelphia. Abraham's mother's eyes had sparkled whenever she recalled the summers in Tarrytown and the gala weddings of her sisters.

In 1932, Connie had another daughter, Charlene Ruth Larson, and, shortly thereafter, Karen met Carroll and his son, Sam. Even though Karen had never thought of starting her family with a teenage son, and despite the reservations of Carroll's father, Karen and Carroll became engaged. Carroll's father died of a heart attack the day after Christmas in 1933, and Karen and her future mother-in-law, Naomi Lee Light, became close.

After her graduation from Hollins in the spring of 1934, Karen and Carroll were married in Tarrytown, New York. Next, the new family moved to Alhambra, California, and Carroll started working as an engineer for Hughes Aircraft. Abraham was born on March 15, 1936, and his sister, Naomi Karen Light, was born in 1939. Abraham had only the vaguest memories of his half-brother, Sam, who joined the Navy later that year.

## 1940–1960

### Light Family Key Dates

| Date | Name | Event | Location |
|------|------|-------|----------|
| 1941 | Samuel Paul Light | Died | Pearl Harbor, Hawaii |
| 1942 | Louise Beatrice Light | Born | Alhambra, California |
| 1945 | Nathaniel Benjamin Greene | Died | Miami, Florida |
| 1950 | Karen Louise (Connor) Greene | Died | Miami, Florida |
| *1954 | Naomi Lee (Spencer) Light | Died | Brandy Run Farm, Virginia |
| 1957 | Abraham Lee Light | | | |
| | Susan Linda Anthony | Married | Fincastle, Virginia |
| 1958 | Carroll Abraham Light, II | Born | Salem, Virginia |

*Will sample related to event shown.

Samuel Paul Light was killed in the Japanese attack on Pearl Harbor on December 7, 1941. His father's copy of Sam's will was in the file; Sam had left everything to his baby half-sister, Naomi. His father started a college fund for her with the proceeds. Abraham's other sister, Louise Beatrice Light, was born in 1942. Carroll was promoted, and when Abraham was eight, the Light family moved to a larger house in Alhambra.

Karen's father, Nathaniel, sold his business in 1943, and he and his wife, Louise, moved to Miami, Florida. After only two years of retirement, Nathaniel died. He had wisely invested the proceeds from the sale of his business and left a substantial trust, which provided Louise with a generous income until she died in Miami in 1950. After her mother's death, Karen received a one-third interest in the trust, as did her two sisters. Except for trips to Florida, the years after the war were quiet as Karen raised her children and began a career as a free-lance writer.

Abraham's father was 54 when he moved his family back to Brandy Run Farm in Botetourt County, Virginia, following the death of his mother, Naomi Lee Light. (See Figure 4.) Abraham's grandmother was buried in the family cemetery at Brandy Run, as were all the Lights except Samuel. Years later, as Abraham settled his mother's estate, he would remember this time when his father faced a similar duty.

As Carroll became involved in improving Brandy Run, Abraham took agriculture courses at Virginia Polytechnic Institute, where his father had earned his engineering degree. In June of 1957, Abraham married Susan Linda Anthony at the Fincastle Presbyterian Church, and they settled in Salem, Virginia. Abraham worked with his father improving the dairy operation and expanding the apple orchards at Brandy Run while Susan taught elementary school. Carroll bought his sister's share of Brandy Run, but Mary Alice, who never married, continued to live there.

On December 18, 1958, Abraham's son, Carroll Abraham Light, II, was born. Karen, now a grandmother, enjoyed the tranquility at the farm and the companionship of Mary Alice, as her husband and son worked together, and she tended young Carroll.

## 1960–1980

### *Light Family Key Dates*

| Date | Name | Event | Location |
|------|------|-------|----------|
| 1963 | Naomi Karen Light<br>Robert William Cotswold | Married | Madison, Wisconsin |
| 1964 | Karen Beth Cotswold | Born | Madison, Wisconsin |
| 1964 | Louise Beatrice Light<br>Frederick Roger Hale | Married | Brandy Run Farm, Virginia |
| 1965 | Samuel Grice Stull | Died | Philadelphia, Pennsylvania |

*(continued)*

### Light Family Key Dates *(continued)*

| Date | Name | Event | Location |
|------|------|-------|----------|
| 1965 | Charles James Hale | Born | Charlottesville, Virginia |
| *1967 | Rachel Beatrice (Greene) Stull | Died | Philadelphia, Pennsylvania |
| 1968 | Dawn Lee Hale | Born | Charlottesville, Virginia |
| 1969 | Robert William Cotswold | Died | Vietnam |
| 1972 | Naomi Karen (Light) Cotswold Graham Carl White | Married | Richmond, Virginia |

*Will sample related to event shown.

Karen's daughter, Naomi, had finished her studies at the University of Wisconsin when she met and married Robert William Cotswold, a career Army officer, in 1963. Karen's first granddaughter, Karen Beth Cotswold, was born in Madison, Wisconsin, the following year. Also in 1964, Karen's younger daughter, Louise, married Frederick Roger Hale at Brandy Run in an outdoor ceremony. The coupled settled near Charlottesville, where Fred operated an automobile dealership and Charles James Hale, Abraham's nephew, was born in 1965.

Reviewing the file, Abraham read through his mother's copy of her sister's will. (See Figure 5.) Rachel Beatrice Stull, who died in 1967, had no children, and her husband had died two years earlier. Karen, as Rachel's Executor, had settled her estate and received a substantial bequest.

Abraham's second niece, Dawn Lee Hale, was born in Charlottesville in 1968. War intruded on the Light family again in 1969, when Naomi's husband, Robert William Cotswold, was killed in Vietnam. Abraham's sister stayed in Madison, Wisconsin, and, in 1970, named Abraham as contingent Executor and guardian for her daughter, Karen Beth Cotswold. (See Figure 6.) Abraham was glad that Naomi prepared a new will soon after her remarriage in 1972. Naomi and Graham Carl White subsequently moved to Richmond, Virginia.

## 1980–1990

### Light Family Key Dates

| Date | Name | Event | Location |
|------|------|-------|----------|
| 1980 | Carroll Abraham Light, II Jo Anne Stone | Married | Dallas, Texas |
| 1982 | Louise Connor (Greene) Larson | Died | Tarrytown, New York |

*(continued)*

### *Light Family Key Dates* (continued)

| Date | Name | Event | Location |
|------|------|-------|----------|
| 1984 | Linda Lee Light | Born | Salem, Virginia |
| 1984 | Carroll Abraham Light | Died | Brandy Run Farm, Virginia |
| *1987 | Paul Abraham Light | Born | Salem, Virginia |
| *1988 | Karen Louise (Greene) Light | Died | Provo, Utah |
| 1989 | IRS Form 706 for Estate of Karen Louise Light filed by Abraham Lee Light, Executor. | | |
| *1989 | Carroll Abraham Light, II | New will | Salem, Virginia |
| *1989 | Jo Anne Stone Light | New will | Salem, Virginia |
| 1990 | Abraham Lee Light | New will | Salem, Virginia |
| 1990 | Susan Anthony Light | New will | Salem, Virginia |

*Will sample related to event shown.

It was in July 1980 that Abraham and Susan's son, Carroll Abraham Light, II, married Jo Anne Stone. Abraham and Susan helped the newlyweds buy a house just down the street. In 1982, Abraham's aunt, Connie Larson, died in her hometown, Tarrytown, New York.

On April 28, 1984, Abraham became a grandfather when Linda Lee Light was born. Both of Abraham's parents were delighted with their first great-granddaughter. In December, Abraham's father, Carroll, died in his sleep, and Abraham helped his mother settle the estate.

Abraham encouraged his mother to buy a new Mercedes and to travel. On July 11, 1987, his mother's first great-grandson, Paul Abraham Light, was born in Salem. (See Figures 7 and 8.) The following year, as Abraham drove his mother to Dulles Airport, he had no way of knowing that her long-planned trip to Hawaii would end tragically in a field in Utah. (See Figures 9 through 11.)

The process that Abraham followed in settling his mother's estate is outlined in the Executor's Checklist in Chapter 6.

# LAST WILL AND TESTAMENT

I, *Naomi Lee Spencer Light*, resident
of the *County* of *Botetourt* in the State of *Virginia*,
being of sound mind, do make and declare the following to be my LAST WILL AND TESTAMENT
and expressly revoke all my prior wills and codicils and certify that I am not acting under undue
influence, duress or menace.

## I. EXECUTOR

I appoint *Abraham Lee Light, my son*, EXECUTOR
of this my LAST WILL AND TESTAMENT. If this EXECUTOR is unable to serve for any reason,
then I appoint *Mary Alice Light, my Daughter*, EXECUTOR.
The EXECUTOR is empowered to carry out all provisions of this WILL.
The EXECUTOR shall have all statutory powers available under State law.
The EXECUTOR named shall not be required to post surety bond. I direct that no outside appraisal
be made of my estate, unless required for estate tax purposes.

## II. BEQUESTS

*I give my entire estate to my dear son, Abraham Lee Light, and to my beloved daughter, Mary Alice Light, in equal shares. This concludes my Last Will and Testament.*

*Figure 4*

60

# LAST WILL AND TESTAMENT

I, <u>Rachel Beatrice Stull</u>, resident
of the <u>City</u> of <u>Philadelphia</u> in the State of <u>PENNSYLVANIA</u>,
being of sound mind, do make and declare the following to be my LAST WILL AND TESTAMENT
and expressly revoke all my prior wills and codicils and certify that I am not acting under undue
influence, duress or menace.

## I. EXECUTOR

I appoint <u>Karen Louise Light, my sister,</u> EXECUTOR
of this, my LAST WILL AND TESTAMENT. If this EXECUTOR is unable to serve for any reason,
then I appoint <u>Abraham Lee Light, my nephew</u> EXECUTOR.
The EXECUTOR is empowered to carry out all provisions of this WILL.
The EXECUTOR shall have all statutory powers available under State law.
The EXECUTOR named shall not be required to post surety bond.
I direct that no outside appraisal be made of my estate, unless
required for estate tax purposes.

## II. BEQUESTS

I give my house, located at 115 Oak Park Drive in the City of
Philadephia, Pennsylvania, to my sister, Louise Connor Larson.

I give my winter home, located at 2120 Key Biscayne Boulevard
in the City of Miami, Florida, to my sister Louise Connor
Larson.

I give all household items, excepting my jewelry and silver
service, to my sister, Louise Connor Larson.

If my sister, Louise Connor Larson, does not survive me by 180
days, then I give her bequests to her daughters, my nieces,
Susan Elizabeth Reynolds and Charlene Ruth Brown, in equal
shares.

I give Mary Ann Washington, my housekeeper, companion and
friend, the sum of five thousand dollars ($5,000.00) and request
that she provide a home for my cats, Ermine and Silky, as we
discussed together.

I give the sum of ten thousand dollars ($10,000.00) to Hunter
College in Queens, New York to the Library Fund for purchase
of art books.

*Figure 5*

61

I give the sum of five thousand dollars ($5,000.00) to the Philadelphia Art Museum, 608 Main Street, Philadelphia, Pennsylvania for the general purposes of the organization.

I give my church, Westminister Presbyterian Church, 18 Society Hill Place, Philadelphia, Pennsylvania the sum of ten thousand dollars ($10,000.00).

I give the American Cancer Society, 1026 Fifth Avenue, New York, New York the sum of ten thousand dollars ($10,000.00) for the purpose of continuing cancer research.

I give my jewelry and silver services to my beloved sister, Karen Louise Light.  I give all the rest of my entire estate, except for the above specific bequests, to my sister, Karen Louise Light, including my one third ownership in the NBG 30 year trust established November 6, 1945, and all cash and securities.

If my sister Karen Louise Light, does not survive me by 180 days, then I give her bequests to her children, Abraham Lee Light, Naomi Karen Cotswold and Louise Beatrice Hale, in equal shares, per stirpes.

This ends my Last Will and Testament

*Figure 5* *(continued)*

# LAST WILL AND TESTAMENT

I, _____ Naomi Karen Cotswold _____ , resident
of the ___ City ___ of _____ Madison _____ in the State of _____ WISCONSIN _____ ,
being of sound mind, do make and declare the following to be my LAST WILL AND TESTAMENT
and expressly revoke all my prior wills and codicils and certify that I am not acting under undue
influence, duress or menace.

## I. EXECUTOR

I appoint _____ Louise Beatrice Hale, my sister, _____ EXECUTOR
of this my LAST WILL AND TESTAMENT. If this EXECUTOR is unable to serve for any reason,
then I appoint _____ Abraham Lee Light, my brother, _____ EXECUTOR.
The EXECUTOR is empowered to carry out all provisions of this WILL.
The EXECUTOR shall have all statutory powers available under State law.
The EXECUTOR named shall not be required to post surety bond. I direct that no outside appraisal
be made of my estate, unless required for estate tax purposes.
I direct that my Executor see that I am buried in the Light family
cemetery located on Brandy Run Farm, in Botetourt County, Virginia.

## II. BEQUESTS

I give my entire estate to my beloved daughter, Karen Beth
Cotswold, with the exception of the following three bequests.

    1.  To my dear sister, Louise Beatrice Hale, I give my
diamond and sapphire dinner ring.

    2.  To my dear brother, Abraham Lee Light, I give my 1965
Ford Mustang Convertible, SN-Q4697216-K.

    3.  I give the sum of five hundred dollars ($500.00)
to my church, Saint James Episcopal Church, 117 Shady
Lane, Madison, Wisconsin.

I direct my Executor to be certain that my life insurance
policy proceeds fund the trust to be administered by the
First Bank and Trust Company of Madison, Wisconsin, in
accord with the trust agreement, dated April 15, 1970.

I appoint my sister, Louise Beatrice Hale, as guardian of
my daughter, Karen Beth Cotswold, until she attains her
majority.  If my sister, Louise Beatrice Hale, does not
survive me, then I appoint my brother Abraham Lee Light,
as guardian of my daughter, Karen Beth Cotswold, until she
attains her majority.

This concludes this my Last Will and Testament.

*Figure 6*

63

# CODICIL

I, _____ Abraham Lee Light _____ , resident

of the ___ City ___ of ___ Salem ___ in the State of

___ VIRGINIA ___ , being of sound mind, do make and declare this codicil to

be my LAST WILL AND TESTAMENT dated ___ June 26 ___ , 19 85 and

certify that I am not acting under undue influence, duress or menace.


I hereby add this additional specific bequest:

I give to my grandson, Paul Abraham Light, the sum of five
thousand dollars ($5,000.00).


In all other respects I ratify and confirm my Will and in witness whereof, I have hereunto set

my hand this ___ First ___ day of ___ October ___ , 19 87 .

*Abraham Lee Light*
*(Testator signature)*

This codicil to the LAST WILL AND TESTAMENT of ___ Abraham Lee Light .

was signed and declared to be his/~~her~~ codicil to his/~~her~~ LAST WILL AND TESTAMENT in our presence

at his/~~her~~ request and in his/~~her~~ presence and the presence of each other as witnesses on this _____

___ First ___ day of ___ October ___ , 19 87 .

*Arnold Raymond Fireston*     116 Maple Dr., Salem Va.
*(Witness signature)*           *(Address)*

*Robert James Townsend*     604 West Main St. Salem, Virginia
*(Witness signature)*           *(Address)*

_____     _____
*(Witness signature)*           *(Address)*

*Figure 7*

64

# CODICIL
# SELF-PROVING CERTIFICATE

State of _____VIRGINIA_____

~~County~~/City of _____Salem_____

Before me, the undersigned authority, on this day personally appeared

_____Abraham Lee Light_____

*Testator* _____Arnold Raymond Firestone_____

*Witness* _____Robert James Townsend_____

*Witness* _____

*Witness* _____

known to me to be the Testator and Witnesses, respectively, whose names are signed to the attached or foregoing instrument and, all of these persons being by me first duly sworn, _____

_____Abraham Lee Light_____ , the testator, declared to me and to the witnesses in my presence that said instrument is a codicil to his/~~her~~ LAST WILL AND TESTAMENT dated _____June 26_____ , 19 __85__ , and that he/~~she~~ had willingly signed or directed another to sign the codicil for him/~~her~~, and executed it in the presence of said witnesses as his/~~her~~ free and voluntary act for the purposes therein expressed; that said witnesses stated before me that the foregoing codicil was executed and acknowledged by the testator as a codicil to his/~~her~~ LAST WILL AND TESTAMENT in the presence of said witnesses who, in his/~~her~~ presence and at his/~~her~~ request, and in the presence of each other, did subscribe their names thereto as attesting witnesses on the day of the date of said codicil, and that the testator, at the time of the execution of said codicil was of sound and disposing mind and memory.

*(Witness signature)*

_____ _____
*(Testator signature)* *(Witness signature)*

_____
*(Witness signature)*

Subscribed, sworn and acknowledged before me by

_____Abraham Lee Light_____ , the Testator,

and subscribed and sworn before me by_____Arnold Raymond Firestone_____

_____and Robert James Townsend_____

_____ , Witnesses,

this _____First_____ day of _____October_____ , 19 __87__ A.D.

Signed: _____
Notary Public

My Commission Expires: _____5-16-91_____

(Seal)

*Figure 8*

65

# LAST WILL AND TESTAMENT

I, _____Karen Louise Light_____ , resident
of the ____County____ of ____Botetourt____ in the State of __VIRGINIA__ ,
being of sound mind, do make and declare the following to be my LAST WILL AND TESTAMENT
and expressly revoke all my prior wills and codicils and certify that I am not acting under undue
influence, duress or menace.

## I. EXECUTOR

I appoint _____Abraham Lee Light, my son_____ EXECUTOR
of this, my LAST WILL AND TESTAMENT. If this EXECUTOR is unable to serve for any reason,

then I appoint _____Louise Beatrice Hale, my daughter,_____ EXECUTOR.
The EXECUTOR is empowered to carry out all provisions of this WILL.
The EXECUTOR shall have all statutory powers available under State law.
The EXECUTOR named shall not be required to post surety bond. I
direct that no outside appraisal be made of my estate, unless
required for estate tax purposes.
The EXECUTOR shall receive the sum of $35,000.00 as compensation.

## II. BEQUESTS

I give my farmland in Botetourt County, Virginia, Parcels
104-1178, 104-1179 and 104-1180, to my three beloved children,
Abraham Lee Light, Naomi Karen White and Louise Beatrice Hale
in equal shares, per stirpes.

I give Brandy Run Farm in Botetourt County, Virginia, Parcels
101-4711, 101-4712, 101-4713 and 102-1008, to my four beloved
grandchildren, Carroll Abraham Light, II, Karen Beth Cotswold,
Charles James Hale and Dawn Lee Hale, in equal shares, per
stirpes.

I give ownership of Patent US-4891086 (Expiration date April
20, 2011) and all royalty rights thereto, to my sister-in-law,
Mary Alice Light.

I give my Steinway baby grand piano to my niece, Charlene Ruth
Brown, per stirpes.

I give my collection of first edition books and the walnut
bookcase housing them, which is located in the study at Brandy
Run Farm, to my niece, Susan Elizabeth Reynolds, per stirpes.

*Figure 9*

66

I give my oil painting, "Mountain Morning", painted by C. F. Bransky, to my good friend, Miriam Rogers Steele.

I give the sum of five thousand dollars ($5,000.00) to Hollins College, Hollins, Virginia for the general scholarship fund.

I give the sum of two thousand five hundred dollars ($2,500.00) to the Roanoke Chapter of the American Red Cross, 312 Church Avenue, Roanoke, Virginia for the general purposes of the organization.

I give my dear son, Abraham Lee Light, all my livestock and farm equipment located at Brandy Run Farm. I give my son, Abraham Lee Light, my 1960 Ford Convertible, Serial Number 06059581CJ and all my shares (100) of C.A.L., Ltd. stock.

I give my dear daughter, Louise Beatrice Hale, my 1984 Mercedes Benz 300 SD Sedan, Serial Number 1QR6785234B.

I give my dear daughter, Naomi Karen White, my LKG monogrammed silverware and all sterling silver serving pieces.

I give all my shares of AT&T, Pacific Gas & Light and IBM stock and all my personal and household personal property, excepting cash accounts, to my beloved daughters, Naomi Karen White and Louise Beatrice Hale in equal shares, per stirpes.

All cash accounts and the entire residue of my estate, I give to my beloved son, Abraham Lee Light, and direct that my Executor take further action regarding the settling of my estate in accord with my Letter of Instructions, dated March 1, 1985, attached to this document as we discussed.

To the members of my family, I wish to state my love for and pride in them all and express my desire that my great-grandchildren be told the background of their family and roots. With best wishes and hope for the future, I conclude this, my Last Will and Testament, at this point.

*Figure 9 (continued)*

# WILL
# SELF-PROVING CERTIFICATE

State of ___VIRGINIA___

County/City of ___Botetourt___

Before me, the undersigned authority, on this day personally appeared

___Karen Louise Light___
_Testator_

___Phillip Roy Jamison___
_Witness_

___Emily Jane Jamison___
_Witness_

_____
_Witness_

known to me to be the Testator and Witnesses, respectively, whose names are signed to the attached or foregoing instrument and, all of these persons being by me first duly sworn, _____

___Karen Louise Light___ , the testator, declared to me and to the witnesses in my presence that said instrument is ~~his~~/her LAST WILL AND TESTAMENT and that ~~he~~/she had willingly signed or directed another to sign the same for ~~him~~/her, and executed it in the presence of said witnesses as ~~his~~/her free and voluntary act for the purposes therein expressed; that said witnesses stated before me that the foregoing will was executed and acknowledged by the testator as ~~his~~/her LAST WILL AND TESTAMENT in the presence of said witnesses who, in ~~his~~/her presence and at ~~his~~/her request, and in the presence of each other, did subscribe their names thereto as attesting witnesses on the day of the date of said will, and that the testator, at the time of the execution of said will was over the age of eighteen years and of sound and disposing mind and memory.

_Karen Louise Light_
(Testator signature)

_Phillip Roy Jamison_
(Witness signature)

_Emily Jane Jamison_
(Witness signature)

Subscribed, sworn and acknowledged before me by

___Karen Louise Light___ , the Testator,

and subscribed and sworn before me by___Phillip Roy Jamison___

___and Emily Jane Jamison___

_____ , Witnesses,

this ___twelth___ day of ___March___ , 19 ___85___ A.D.

Signed: _Ms. Notary Public_
Notary Public

My Commission Expires: ___3-31-87___

(Seal)

*Figure 10*

68

# LETTER OF INSTRUCTIONS

March 1, 1985

To my Executor,

My husband Carroll and I discussed passing on the family farm many times before he died. The distribution of shares of ownership is set out in the will. I direct that the balance of cash accounts, after deductions of cash bequests and the agreed upon Executor's fee, be applied to estate taxes due. I direct that the commercial building, Lot 7, Blocks 131-135 in the City of Salem be sold and the proceeds be applied to estate taxes due. In the event that insufficient funds to pay all estate taxes will remain after my specific bequests have been made, I direct that my Executor arrange a loan for the balance needed, to be secured by the parcels of farmland 104-1178, 104-1179, 104-1180 located in Botetourt County, Virginia, prior to final transfer of encumbered title interests. I further direct my Executor to continue current farm lease payments to all owners of the farmland and Brandy Run Farm according to their share of ownership as long as the Brandy Run dairy farm and orchard is under family management. The lease payment income should offset most of the estate tax loan payment. I direct that this plan be followed by my children as I recognize that it will cause the least financial impact and that they all are of more than adequate means to carry it out.

I direct that my Executor transfer the patent rights to Carroll's fiber-optic switching control device to his sister, Mary Alice Light, and to close C.A.L., Ltd., the private corporation administering the royalty rights. I recognize that, if Mary Alice Light dies before me, the bequest will be adeemed, and revert to Abraham Lee Light. In that case, the instruction to close C.A.L.,Ltd. does not apply.

If in the division of my personal and household goods, my daughters should disagree, the matter is to be resolved by a flip of a coin, supervised by the Executor.

With love,

*Karen Louise Light*

Karen Louise Light

March 1, 1985

*Figure 11*

## *Looking Ahead*

Because Abraham and his mother had discussed her wishes frequently and he was thoroughly familiar with the family's financial situation, he was able to settle her estate without encountering any unforeseen difficulties. Drawing on his experience as Executor, Abraham talked to his son, Carroll, and Carroll's wife, Jo Anne, about the importance of their wills and suggested how his grandchildren's interests might be protected. (See Figures 12 through 14.) He now understood how family wealth was built and was grateful for the foresight of his parents and grandparents. His family had been through a wide range of experiences, and the future was bright. Abraham completed his family history notes and gave Susan the names and dates to fill in on copies of the family tree that would become Christmas gifts for all of Carroll and Karen's descendants.

# LAST WILL AND TESTAMENT

I, _____ Carroll Abraham Light, II _____ , resident

of the __ City __ of ____ Salem ____ in the State of __ VIRGINIA __ ,

being of sound mind, do make and declare the following to be my LAST WILL AND TESTAMENT and expressly revoke all my prior wills and codicils and certify that I am not acting under undue influence, duress or menace.

## I. EXECUTOR

I appoint _____ Jo Anne Stone Light, my wife, _____ EXECUTOR of this my LAST WILL AND TESTAMENT. If this EXECUTOR is unable to serve for any reason,

then I appoint _____ Abraham Lee Light, my father _____ EXECUTOR.

The EXECUTOR is empowered to carry out all provisions of this WILL.

The EXECUTOR shall have all statutory powers available under State law.

The EXECUTOR named shall not be required to post surety bond. I direct that no outside appraisal be made of my estate, unless required for estate tax purposes.

## II. BEQUESTS

I give my entire estate to my beloved wife, Jo Anne Stone Light, with the exception of my share of ownership of Brandy Run Farm (Parcels 101-4711, 101-4712, 101-4713, 102-1008) located in Botetourt County, Virginia, which I give to my dear daughter, Linda Lee Light, and my dear son, Paul Abraham Light, in equal shares.

If my wife, Jo Anne Stone Light, does not survive me by more than 180 days, then I give my entire estate to my daughter, Linda Lee Light, and my son, Paul Abraham Light, in equal shares and appoint Abraham Lee Light, my father, as guardian of my children until they attain their majority.

This ends my Last Will and Testament.

*Figure 12*

# LAST WILL AND TESTAMENT

I, _____Jo Anne Stone Light_____ , resident
of the __City__ of ____Salem_____ in the State of __VIRGINIA____ ,
being of sound mind, do make and declare the following to be my LAST WILL AND TESTAMENT
and expressly revoke all my prior wills and codicils and certify that I am not acting under undue
influence, duress or menace.

## I. EXECUTOR

I appoint _____Carroll Abraham Light, II, my husband__ EXECUTOR
of this my LAST WILL AND TESTAMENT. If this EXECUTOR is unable to serve for any reason,
then I appoint _____Abraham Lee Light, my father-in-law,__ EXECUTOR.
The EXECUTOR is empowered to carry out all provisions of this WILL.
The EXECUTOR shall have all statutory powers available under State law.
The EXECUTOR named shall not be required to post surety bond. I direct that no outside appraisal
be made of my estate, unless required for estate tax purposes.

## II. BEQUESTS

I give my entire estate to my beloved husband, Carroll
Abraham Light, II. If my husband, Carroll Abraham Light, II,
dies before me, then I give my entire estate to my dear
daughter, Linda Lee Light and my dear son, Paul Abraham Light,
in equal shares and appoint Abraham Lee Light, my father-in-law,
as guardian of my children until they attain their majority.

This ends my Last Will and Testament.

*Figure 13*

# WILL
# SELF-PROVING CERTIFICATE

State of _VIRGINIA_

County/City of _Salem_

Before me, the undersigned authority, on this day personally appeared

_Jo Anne Stone Light_

*Testator* _Ralph Peter Stanley_

*Witness* _Martha Virginia Stanley_

*Witness* _____

*Witness* _____

known to me to be the Testator and Witnesses, respectively, whose names are signed to the attached or foregoing instrument and, all of these persons being by me first duly sworn, _Jo Anne Stone Light_ , the testator, declared to me and to the witnesses in my presence that said instrument is his/her LAST WILL AND TESTAMENT and that he/she had willingly signed or directed another to sign the same for him/her, and executed it in the presence of said witnesses as his/her free and voluntary act for the purposes therein expressed; that said witnesses stated before me that the foregoing will was executed and acknowledged by the testator as his/her LAST WILL AND TESTAMENT in the presence of said witnesses who, in his/her presence and at his/her request, and in the presence of each other, did subscribe their names thereto as attesting witnesses on the day of the date of said will, and that the testator, at the time of the execution of said will was over the age of eighteen years and of sound and disposing mind and memory.

_Jo Anne Stone Light_
(Testator signature)

_Ralph Peter Stanley_ (Witness signature)

_Martha Virginia Stanley_ (Witness signature)

Subscribed, sworn and acknowledged before me by

_Jo Anne Stone Light_ , the Testator,

and subscribed and sworn before me by _Ralph Peter Stanley_

_and Martha Virginia Stanley_

_____ , Witnesses,

this _seventeenth_ day of _February_ , 19 _89_ A.D.

Signed: _Ms Notary Public_

Notary Public

My Commission Expires: _5-16-91_

(Seal)

*Figure 14*

73

CHAPTER *6*

# Executor's Guide

Your Executor is responsible for administering your estate and carrying out the terms of your will. The Executor will work closely with your family and beneficiaries during the probate process and become familiar with financial and personal details of your estate. Naming your spouse, major beneficiary, a relative, or a friend as Executor can save expense to the estate and help maintain privacy. The duties of the Executor are not difficult and normally require only routine recordkeeping and accounting ability. Your chosen Executor can employ professional assistance for specific probate tasks if needed. Careful and efficient administration by the Executor conserves your estate for your beneficiaries.

The duties of the Executor, though not complicated, require care, time, and attention to detail. Compensating the person you've chosen to settle your estate is usually unnecessary if you've named your spouse or other major beneficiary as Executor. If you name someone other than a primary beneficiary to settle your estate, you should discuss compensation and be sure that the named person consents to serve. Your Executor should be a responsible, trustworthy person who has concern for your family, beneficiaries, and estate. If no one close to you is able to act as your Executor, you should consider your options carefully. Most trust officers of financial institutions, attorneys, and other professionals offer Executor services on a fee basis. Before naming a professional Executor, discuss your estate plan with the prospective appointee, and agree to a fee schedule in advance.

## Appointing an Executor

The Executor of an estate is nominated in the will of the Testator and, upon approval, appointed by the court of probate. "Letters testamentary" are issued to the Executor as official proof of appointment. After formal appointment, the Executor must fulfill the duties prescribed by law and, to the extent possible, carry out the terms of the will. The duties and powers of the Executor are defined by state statute unless limited or expanded in the will. The Executor's role involves acting as the agent of the Testator to pay debts, expenses, and taxes for which the estate is liable and to collect any debts, fees, or property due the estate. After debts, expenses, and taxes have been paid, the remaining property is given to the beneficiaries according to the terms of the will. With court approval, after all estate property has been distributed and accounted for, the estate is closed. Settling an estate is usually not difficult or costly, although patience and careful attention to detail are necessary. If certain tasks require skills and expertise beyond the capabilities of the Executor, he or she may obtain professional assistance. Saving expenses to the estate, which conserves assets for the beneficiaries, is a primary concern of the Executor.

## The Appointment of an Administrator

Much of the information presented here about Executors applies also to those who petition the court to act as Administrator of an intestate estate. The Administrator and Executor perform similar functions in settling an estate, the primary difference being that the Executor distributes the estate according to the Testator's will, whereas the Administrator must distribute the estate according to state intestate succession law.

A member of the family of a person who dies intestate usually seeks appointment, although others with an interest in the estate may also apply. If no applicants are accepted by the court, or no one applies, the court appoints an Administrator, usually a local attorney. The Administrator is entitled, by law, to reasonable compensation, usually totaling 3 to 5 percent of the appraised value of the estate.

An intestate estate is administered according to state statutes, usually with close court supervision. The Administrator must post a surety bond, obtainable through a local bonding agent or company, to protect the assets of the estate.

## *Conserving and Collecting Assets*

The estate of the Testator consists of all the real and personal property owned at the time of death. The duty of the Executor is to collect and conserve that property and, after all estate expenses have been paid, to distribute the remainder according to the terms of the will. Upon appointment, the Executor should promptly identify and secure all estate assets.

An inventory of the estate of the Testator will be needed during the probate process. It is the Executor's duty to exercise reasonable diligence in locating all estate assets. If the Executor is the spouse or primary beneficiary of the Testator, the type, location, and value of all assets are usually known. If the Executor is unfamiliar with the estate, a complete search for all real and personal assets will be necessary. Inquiries of relatives and friends, along with careful review of the records of the Testator, should locate most assets. A thorough search of records and receipts can reveal bank deposits, rental storage units, and other assets of the Testator. Any professional or family advisers may also be useful sources of information and assistance. After all estate assets are located and secured, the Executor should list them with adequate detail as to type of asset, location, and value. The completed inventory provides the basis for valuing the estate for state and federal estate tax purposes. Careful recordkeeping simplifies the tasks of accounting and tax filing.

As estate assets are collected, they must be conserved and protected. A separate bank account, with its own Federal Employer Identification Number (FEIN), should be opened in the name of the estate as soon as practicable. Any monies, proceeds from liquidated assets, or benefits due the Testator and estate are recorded and deposited in the estate account, and legitimate estate expenses are paid from that account. Do not neglect to file for Social Security death benefits and, if the decedent is eligible to receive them, Veterans Administration, civil service, and/or Railroad Retirement death benefits. If substantial cash assets are available, an interest-bearing account should be considered. Interest earned by the estate may be subject to federal and state income taxes. A separate account, with accurate and detailed records, is also useful in completing any tax returns for the estate.

## *Types of Administration and Accounting*

The Executor must carry out the duties of administering the estate according to state requirements. Most states have both supervised and unsupervised administration of an estate, with the probate court determining the type of administration available to the Executor. The court, when deciding the type of administration, considers the nature and extent of the estate, its value, and the skills and abilities of the Executor. Fully supervised administration requires the Executor to seek court approval for almost all actions taken in the probate process. A complete inventory of estate assets, valued by court-approved appraisers, and a full audit of accounts may be required before debts are paid or any property is distributed to beneficiaries.

Unsupervised administration allows the Executor to perform many, if not all, probate tasks without prior court approval. The time and effort required of the Executor is minimized when this type of administration is used. The probate court determines the type of administration available to the Executor. Texas requires the use of the term "independent Executor" in the will for unsupervised administration.

# Debts and Creditors

Creditors' claims against the estate, funeral expenses, and bills owed by the Testator must be examined for validity, reasonableness, and accuracy by the Executor. Under unsupervised administration, payment of many claims may be made by the Executor without specific court approval. In some states, the claims must be filed directly to the court and, upon approval, paid by the Executor. Each claim should be listed with the basis of the claim, the amount, the date due, and the name and address of the claimant noted. Monthly billing statements from credit card companies, retail stores, or others are usually valid claims of this type. Any time or demand notes due a bank or other financial institution, documented loans from individuals, and auto loans are included as well. Rent or lease payments owed by the Testator must be paid, and the Executor should notify rental agents/lessors immediately if property is vacated.

The Testator's creditors must be informed, by letter or public notice, of the opening of the estate and given the opportunity to present legitimate claims. In a few states, creditors must be contacted by letter or notice in the mail. The Executor must conduct a search for evidence of debt and notify the creditors within a time specified by the court. Public notice is a more common practice, and the process required to notify creditors is similar in most states. A notice is published in local newspapers informing anyone having a claim against the estate of the Testator's death and the opening of the estate for probate. The creditors are given a specific number of days to file their claims and any related documents. The exact requirements for this notice and the number of times it must be published can be obtained from the court of probate. If a creditor fails to file a claim in the period of time required by law, there is no legal obligation to pay the debt. In such a case, payment may be made at the discretion of the Executor/Administrator. If the assets of the Testator are insufficient to pay all the debts owed, they must be paid in an order determined by state law. Preferred claims are defined by state laws and must be paid before all others. These claims usually include funeral expenses, estate administration expenses, fees, and outstanding taxes due. It is important to obtain a receipt for every claim paid from the estate. The remaining debts of the Testator are usually prorated and paid to the extent possible. If there is any question regarding a creditor's claim, the court should rule on its validity.

Personal property of the Testator may be encumbered by a debt or collateral situation. Release of such property may require the Executor to pay the balance outstanding from the estate assets. Repair bills for an automobile and redemption of pawned jewelry are typical examples. Rents on storage units or garages that are in arrears must be paid to secure the contents. Tools, lawn equipment, autos, boats, or other property lent to friends and any art or collections on loan for display should be secured as soon as practicable.

## Real Property

Real estate and real property interests are the major assets of many estates. Real property owned by the Testator entirely and given to a specific beneficiary in the will must be maintained and insured to protect its value until title passes to the beneficiary. In the case of unimproved land, little if any maintenance is required, and insurance, with the possible exception of liability, is usually unnecessary. A house, building, or other structure must be protected with adequate insurance and should be maintained and secured. Payment of utilities and taxes must be made when due, as well as any homeowner or property association fees, regular maintenance charges, or other legitimate expenses. A vacant, neglected structure is a likely target for thieves and vandals and should be properly secured and maintained to prevent deterioration.

Ownership interests in real property may include partial interests in rental property, commercial buildings, or vacation property. In some states, "interval-ownership" (time-share) rights are also considered as real property and may be disposed of in a will. The Executor should obtain the originals or copies of all deeds or other title evidence to determine the ownership interest of the Testator.

The Testator may also own real estate as a joint tenant, tenant by the entirety, or tenant in common. Upon the death of a joint tenant with right of survivorship, or a tenant by the entirety, the property transfers to the surviving spouse or joint tenant, with no action required of the Executor. Though this property is not a part of the probate estate, the Executor must list the value of property transferred in this manner as part of the Testator's taxable estate. Property held as a tenant in common is owned individually and disposed of in the will. The Executor must list the interest held by the Testator as a tenant in common as an asset of the estate and distribute it under the terms of the will.

Liabilities against real property must be considered by the Executor in determining the true value of the property for tax purposes. Liabilities against real estate may include mortgages, home equity credit lines, reverse mortgages, life estates, and any taxes due against the property. Mortgage payments are usually continued by the Executor to allow the beneficiary flexibility in deciding whether to keep the existing mortgage, secure a new one, or sell the property. Other liabilities may have to be paid by the estate or beneficiary before the property can be transferred. Real estate owned by the Testator that is not in the state of residence requires the appointment of an ancillary representative who is a resident of the state in which the property is located. This person is responsible for the actual administration of the property and makes sure that appropriate state taxes are paid. The Executor must list out-of-state property when filing federal estate tax forms and include the value when determining whether the estate exceeds the $600,000 exemption limit.

The Executor may, upon direction of the Testator and approval by the court, sell real property and distribute the proceeds as directed in the will. State laws differ in the authority given an Executor to dispose of real property. In some states, the Executor must have the approval of the court and beneficiaries before real estate is sold, while others allow the Executor to sell with few restrictions. If the Testator contracted to sell property prior to death, the Executor is usually required to complete the contract on the Testator's behalf and to account for the proceeds. It is always advisable for the Executor to check with the court of probate before offering to sell real estate.

The value of real property owned by the Testator has a significant impact on the amount of federal and state taxes the estate will be liable for. In some situations, the Executor may be required to obtain a professional appraisal of the real assets for tax purposes. The Executor should carefully record and list the value of all property of the Testator, including nonprobate assets. Transactions regarding real property should be approved by the court of probate and the beneficiaries of the Testator.

## Business Interests

Business interests of the Testator are usually transferred by a buy-sell agreement, stock transfer, or some other arrangement set out in advance. Because of potential personal liability, the Executor must exercise extreme care if business interests are included in the will of the Testator. The Executor, under most state laws, cannot continue business operations unless specifically authorized to do so in the will of the Testator. If no authorization is given, most states require the Executor to conserve the business for only as long as required to liquidate it. Under these circumstances, any continuance of the business must be done with court approval. If specific authorization is given to continue the business, the Executor is responsible for due care and operation of the business in a reasonable manner. Operation of a business is usually time-consuming and, in many situations, exposes the Executor to personal liability. Before taking any action regarding the Testator's business interests, the Executor should seek approval of the court and beneficiaries.

## Distribution/Accounting

After assembling and securing the Testator's property and paying all debts, expenses, and taxes, the Executor may distribute the estate. If the estate is properly disposed of by the Testator's will and is adequate to fulfill all bequests, this task can be simple. The Executor distributes the bequests and obtains receipts from the beneficiaries. Many states allow estates to be distributed without formal accounting when the beneficiaries are in agreement. Most courts also allow small estates, typically $10,000 or less, to be settled without formal accounting. Informal distribution is a simple procedure that avoids the additional expense and time required by a formal accounting.

If a formal accounting is called for, the Executor must follow state and local laws. The estate must be audited and all interested parties notified of the date and place of filing of the account. At the time of the audit, creditors, beneficiaries, or others with objections may be heard by the court. If the court approves of the audited account, a schedule of distribution is prepared, and the property is given to the designated beneficiary(ies). The Executor must have receipts from all beneficiaries before being released from his or her duties.

## Taxes

The Executor is responsible for filing all federal and state tax forms on behalf of the Testator and estate. Care must be taken to determine the tax liability and appropriate filing dates. Federal tax liabilities may include income taxes owed by the Testator and, if any income is earned, by the estate as well. Federal estate tax is due if the total amount of the taxable estate exceeds $600,000.

The taxable estate of the Testator includes the probate assets and other taxable assets. Taxable gifts made after 1976, joint property and tenant-by-the-entirety interests, and the value of buy-sell agreements are included in the taxable estate. Life insurance proceeds may also be included in the taxable estate. The Executor should have accurate records of the value of the Testator's property, including the nonprobate assets, to determine if the estate is liable for federal estate tax.

State taxes can include income taxes, as well as other taxes related to the transfer of the estate. The state department of taxation and the court of probate can assist the Executor in determining current state estate tax requirements.

## Executor Resources

Many resources are available to the Executor throughout the probate process. The best assistance is provided by the Testator who, if thorough, has left a current will along with complete records and instructions. An Executor should be as informed and aware of the Testator's estate plan as possible, preferably through prior discussion. The location of original documents, especially the will, records, and deeds needed to settle the estate, must be known to the Executor. A current will and adequate direction by the Testator can simplify the Executor's task immensely.

Accountants, appraisers, attorneys, and other professionals may be employed by the Executor in the probate process. Reasonable fees for professional assistance may be paid with estate assets in almost all situations. The Executor may often save expenses to the estate by employing professionals on an hourly basis while personally performing most routine probate tasks.

Personnel of the local court of probate, as public employees, are valuable resources; they can provide the Executor with basic information and other assistance. Developing a good working relationship with court personnel can often be of great value to the Executor during the probate process.

The position of Executor involves a close relationship with the family and friends of the Testator. The support and understanding of those close to the Testator can be especially helpful to the Executor in the probate process. At the same time, personal concern and sensitivity on the part of the Executor can be a great comfort to those who have experienced a loss.

## Reviewing the Executor's Checklist

The checklist on pages 84–87 is intended to provide general guidance for an Executor or Administrator of an estate. Not every task will be necessary for every estate; however, the entire checklist should be reviewed to make sure that nothing is overlooked. You may wish to retain a professional to assist you if the estate is complicated and requires extensive administration. An Executor works with the clerk of the local court throughout the probate process and should direct specific questions to that person, because requirements change over time.

To act efficiently on behalf of the Testator, it is important to have full understanding and knowledge of his or her estate plan. As soon as possible after you have agreed to act as Executor, discuss with the Testator the will, beneficiaries, and any instructions regarding the estate. The addresses and telephone numbers of beneficiaries and the location of assets, property, and other estate components should be noted. Any professional advisers to the Testator for legal, accounting, insurance, tax, or investment services should also be identified. The more information the Executor has about the estate, the easier estate administration becomes. Encourage the Testator to list *all* the relevant information needed to settle the estate. If business interests or other matters requiring continuing administration are involved, be sure to have a clear understanding of the details.

## *Executor's Checklist*

_____ Locate the original of the last will of the Testator and any related documents.

_____ Obtain several copies of the death certificate.

*NOTE:* If no will is found, petition the court to administer the estate.

_____ Submit documents to the clerk of the court having jurisdiction over probate in the locality where the Testator was a legal resident to start the probate process. Refer to the State Summary, Chapter 9, for the name of the court having jurisdiction over probate.

Court: _____

Address: _____

_____

Clerk: _____

Phone: (     ) _____

_____ Have court confirm appointment as Executor.

*NOTE:* If nonresident, make arrangement for resident personal representative, if required.

_____ Post surety bond, if required.

_____ Obtain letters of administration from court.

_____ Elect unsupervised or small estate status, if available.

_____ Request that court confirm appointment of guardian(s).

_____ Arrange for ancillary probate administration of property located in other states.

_____ Consider the surviving spouse's right of election.

_____ Notify all interested persons of the opening of the probate process.

# Executor's Checklist *(continued)*

_____    Arrange for notice of creditors as required in state.

_____    Apply for Federal Employer Identification Number (FEIN) for estate.

_____    Open bank account(s) for estate.

_____    Contact Testator's employer for unpaid salary and benefits, such as life insurance.

_____    File claims for life insurance.

_____    File for any Social Security, civil service, Veterans Administration, or other death and pension benefits.

_____    Identify and expedite transfer of property not subject to probate (trusts, jointly held property).

_____    Provide funds for allowable living expenses to surviving spouse and dependents with approval of local court.

_____    Notify utilities, post office, creditors, and so on of Testator's death and transfer accounts to survivors or estate as appropriate.

_____    Open and inventory all safe-deposit boxes; transfer contents of estate safe-deposit box, if necessary.

*NOTE:* Some states require that a representative of the state be present at the opening of the decedent's safe-deposit box.

_____    Review financial records and recent tax returns of Testator.

_____    Prepare list of all beneficiaries, including Social Security numbers.

_____    Prepare preliminary estimate of value of estate.

_____    Appraise estate assets for a "date of death" valuation.

_____    Engage professional appraisers, if required by court or for tax purposes.

*(continued)*

## *Executor's Checklist (continued)*

_____ Check with court for any claims filed against estate.

_____ Inspect all real estate and review mortgages, leases, property insurance policies, and so forth.

_____ Arrange for management of real property located in other states.

_____ Make arrangements for such special concerns as business interests and ongoing farming operations.

_____ Collect all property belonging, or owed, to the estate.

_____ Prepare and file Testator's personal federal and state income tax returns for portion of last year of life.

*NOTE:* Qualifying widow/widower status is available if dependent children live with surviving spouse.

_____ Determine cash needs of estate.

_____ Arrange sale of estate property, if required.

_____ Pay all valid claims, bills, and expenses, with court approval if required.

_____ Prepare complete detailed inventory and appraisal of entire estate and file it with the court, with copies to major beneficiaries.

_____ Prepare and file federal and state estate income tax returns for period of administration.

_____ File federal and state estate tax returns, if applicable.

*NOTE:* A certified copy of the will must be attached to estate tax returns.

_____ Obtain court authorization to pay professional fees, if applicable.

_____ Distribute all assets as set out in will.

*(continued)*

## Executor's Checklist (continued)

_____    Prepare final account of estate assets and distribution with receipts, and file it with the court.

_____    Close estate, and obtain documents from court indicating completion of Executor's duties.

_____    Retain copies of all records in a personal file for at least three years.

# CHAPTER 7

# Taxes

## Background

Because of the $600,000 federal estate tax exemption and the unlimited marital deduction, most estates face no federal estate tax liability at this time. When preparing an estate plan, you should note the value of real estate and other assets that may be included in your taxable estate. Appreciation, especially in real property values, can significantly affect your taxable estate. If your estate is approaching the exemption level, you should consider additional estate planning methods that can lower tax liabilities. Married couples should calculate the combined value of their taxable estates when making estate planning decisions. Federal estate taxes, marital deductions, taxable estate components, and other related topics are discussed in this chapter. State taxes, including state estate tax, income tax, credit estate tax, and inheritance taxes are also discussed and explained.

Death and taxes have been linked since Caesar Augustus created the first estate tax, set at 5 percent, to maintain the armies of the Roman Empire. The Roman system was in effect in Britain until 1066, when the Norman invasion introduced principles of French feudal law.

In 1540, the Statute of Wills was made a part of English Common Law and established methods of distribution of real property as well as different intestate succession criteria. Because this system was based on real property, which was of primary importance in the agrarian-based society, the marital rights of the dower and curtesy and the principle of homestead were established. English Common Law was the starting point of most of the estate laws of the United States.

French legal influence is evident in the state laws of Louisiana, a community-property state, where a parent may not completely disinherit a child. Most of the other community-property states were influenced by Spanish legal practice, which was similar to that of the French.

Another factor affecting the estate laws was the period in which they were enacted and subsequently revised, which depends to some extent on the time of statehood. Laws enacted in different centuries and decades naturally differ, as do laws that result from longer or shorter periods of testing, experience, and revision. With all these different components and legal traditions, it is not surprising that requirements relating to wills, estates, probate, intestate succession, and estate and inheritance taxes have varied greatly from state to state. Since about 1900, however, the federal taxation system and promotion of various model legislative acts dealing with such things as simultaneous death, probate, and living wills have worked to produce more uniformity in state laws.

Recently, the trend toward greater uniformity has accelerated. Extensive revision of federal estate and gift taxation law was initiated in 1981, and in 1987 new provisions were fully phased in. One result is that all states base their estate tax on the federal schedule of credit for state death taxes. Many states impose additional estate, gift, generation-skip transfer, and inheritance taxes on property passing through the probate process.

## Your Estate

Your estate consists of everything you own or retain a controlling interest in and includes any amounts owed to you (unless uncollectible). Estate components may include:

- Real property.
- Tangible personal property.
- Intangible personal property.
- Intellectual property.
- Life insurance proceeds.
- Annuities/pensions (with survivor payments).
- Custodial accounts.
- Debts and sums receivable.

- Business ownership.
- Inheritances paid to your estate.
- Taxable gifts (after 1976).

The total of your estate is known as your gross estate. Your gross estate is reduced by your outstanding liabilities and certain other expenses to calculate your taxable estate. Amounts deductible from the gross estate when the taxable estate is figured are:

- Administration and funeral expenses.
- Claims against the estate.
- Any outstanding obligation to which the property is subject.
- Casualty and theft losses.
- Marital deductions.
- Charitable deductions.

Certain items included in your gross estate, such as custodial accounts, do not pass under the terms of your will and hence are not included in your probate estate. As a result, the values of your gross estate, taxable estate, and probate estate are usually different.

# Federal Taxes

## INCOME TAX

Federal income tax will be due on income received by the Testator during the last year of life. Responsibility for filing the final income tax return falls on the Executor of the estate. The final income tax return is due on the former taxpayer's regular annual schedule. For calendar-year filers, the final return will be due April 15 of the year after death, or later if an extension of time to file is requested and obtained.

It is advisable for the widow or widower to determine whether joint or separate filing status is more advantageous for a final return and to file accordingly. A spouse who remarries during the same tax year as the death of a Testator may not file a final joint return with the deceased. Qualifying widows and widowers (those who provide over half the living costs of a dependent child and do not remarry) may elect to use joint filing status for two years.

When your Executor takes charge of your affairs, a Federal Employer Identification Number (FEIN) is applied for. This number identifies the estate as a distinct entity. Income to the estate, such as interest, dividends, rents, and royalties, is subject to federal income tax if it exceeds $600 during any tax year prior to complete settlement of the estate. Your Executor is responsible for filing the estate income tax return.

Members of the U.S. armed forces who die while on active duty in a combat zone have their income tax liability abated (forgiven) for all tax years since beginning service in the combat zone. If income tax has been paid, a return may be claimed on behalf of the estate. This income tax abatement also applies to death resultant from wounds, disease, or injury incurred in a combat zone (after June 24, 1950). Estates of members of the U.S. armed forces officially listed as missing in action (MIA) are entitled to the same income tax abatement. Both military and civilian employees of the United States who die as a result of a terrorist or military action outside the United States (after November 17, 1978) are also eligible for income tax abatement from the time the fatal wound or injury was incurred. Special forms available from the Department of Defense or the Department of State must accompany the estate's request for income tax abatement.

## ESTATE TAX

Federal estate tax is a tax on the *transfer* of property resultant from death. Currently, if the value of the gross estate at death is less than $600,000, the estate exemption threshold, no federal estate tax will be due. The taxable estate may be reduced below the $600,000 threshold if property passes to a surviving spouse. All property left to a surviving spouse may be deducted from the taxable estate utilizing Schedule M, Bequests, Etc., to Surviving Spouse. This marital deduction is unlimited as to amount and, if used, has the effect of deferring federal estate taxation until the death of the surviving spouse. If you are married and have a sizable estate, you may wish to distribute up to the $600,000 threshold amount to others, with the balance to your spouse. This approach can reduce the total estate tax liability compared to that incurred if all property is given to the surviving spouse and the first $600,000 available exemption is not used. No marital deduction is available to a surviving spouse who is not a U.S. citizen. However, a marital deduction is allowed for property passing in a qualified domestic trust to a surviving alien spouse.

Life insurance proceeds paid to your estate or to your Executor are included in your gross taxable estate for federal estate tax purposes. Further, life insurance proceeds that are not payable to, or for the benefit of, your estate can be included in your federal gross taxable estate if you hold any of the incidents of ownership in the policy on the following list.

- Legal ownership of the policy.
- The power to change beneficiaries.
- The power to revoke an assignment.
- The right to obtain a loan against the policy.
- The right to surrender or cancel the policy.

Rights that are not considered to be incidents of ownership include the right to receive dividends and the right to veto the sale of the policy by the trustee of an irrevocable trust funded by insurance. Careful review of your life insurance policies is necessary to determine federal estate tax implications.

If the total fair market value of the estate assets decreases in the six months after death, the alternate valuation method may also be used to reduce or eliminate federal estate tax liability. The alternate valuation method values property when sold, transferred, or distributed and all undistributed assets at their value six months after the date of death rather than on the actual date of death. The maximum amount by which an estate may be decreased using the alternate valuation method is limited to $750,000.

If a federal estate tax return (IRS Form 706) is required, your Executor must file it within nine months after the actual date of death.

Owners of farms and closely held businesses, when the farm or business real property constitutes a substantial portion of the gross estate, should be aware that their Executors may also elect special-use valuation, basing value on return from use rather than fair market value. Additionally, longer installment payment options for federal estate tax due are available to owners of farms and closely held businesses, subject to various situation-specific requirements.

## GIFT TAX

Federal gift tax is incurred when a "taxable gift" is made. Currently, a taxable gift is the value of any gift to a person in excess of $10,000 in the donor's tax year. Stated conversely, gifts of $10,000 or less are exempt from gift taxes. Previously, gift taxes and estate taxes were reported and collected separately and had different taxation rates. However, congressional action created a unification of these two taxes at a single rate. As a result, taxable gifts made after 1976 must be taken into account when calculating federal estate tax liability. The total amount of adjusted taxable gifts is subtracted from the $600,000 federal estate tax exemption level. If you have made substantial adjusted taxable gifts over the last 18 years, be aware of the lower threshold exemption level available to the estate. Note that qualified transfers, which are amounts paid to an educational organization as tuition or to a health-care institution for medical care on behalf of another, are not considered taxable gifts for tax calculation purposes.

In addition to the reduction of the $600,000 federal estate tax exemption by the amount of adjusted taxable gifts, be aware that generation-skipping transfers are included when figuring the total amount of the taxable estate subject to federal estate tax. Since the general policy regarding federal estate tax is to tax the transfer of property at the point of generational change (normally the death of the surviving spouse), gifts to grandchildren or others at least two generations removed from the Testator are included in the gross estate. If generation-skipping transfers have been included in your estate plan, it is advisable to review the terms and methods in light of current federal estate tax.

# State Taxes

## INCOME TAX

State income tax will be due on income received by the Testator during the last year of life in those states that impose income tax. Filing the state tax return on the former taxpayer's usual tax-year basis is the responsibility of the Executor. Income to the estate above the state's annual minimum will also be subject to a state income tax each tax year until the estate is settled and closed.

## ESTATE TAX

All states impose federal credit estate taxes. Additionally, seven states (Massachusetts, Mississippi, New York, Ohio, Oklahoma, Rhode Island, and South Carolina) impose estate taxes at state-determined rates on the estate after certain deductions. The federal credit estate tax amounts are shown on the following Federal (IRS) Credit for State Death Taxes schedule. The schedule applies to the taxable amount of the estate (currently the federal taxable estate, less $60,000). This method is known as federal credit estate taxation, and it starts with taxable estates in excess of $100,000 (after subtracting the $60,000 deduction).

### Credit for State Death Taxes

| A<br>Taxable Amount<br>Equal to or<br>Over | B<br>Taxable<br>Amount Not<br>Over | C<br>Credit on<br>Amount in<br>Column A | D<br>Rate of Credit on<br>Excess over Amount<br>in Column A (%) |
|---|---|---|---|
| $100,000 | $150,000 | 0 | 0.8 |
| 150,000 | 200,000 | $400 | 1.6 |
| 200,000 | 300,000 | 1,200 | 2.4 |
| 300,000 | 500,000 | 3,600 | 3.2 |
| 500,000 | 700,000 | 10,000 | 4.0 |
| 700,000 | 900,000 | 18,000 | 4.8 |
| 900,000 | 1,100,000 | 27,600 | 5.6 |
| 1,100,000 | 1,600,000 | 38,800 | 6.4 |
| 1,600,000 | 2,100,000 | 70,800 | 7.2 |
| 2,100,000 | 2,600,000 | 106,800 | 8.0 |
| 2,600,000 | 3,100,000 | 146,800 | 8.8 |
| 3,100,000 | 3,600,000 | 190,800 | 9.6 |
| 3,600,000 | 4,100,000 | 238,800 | 10.4 |

*(continued)*

**Credit for State Death Taxes** (continued)

| A<br>Taxable Amount Equal to or Over | B<br>Taxable Amount Not Over | C<br>Credit on Amount in Column A | D<br>Rate of Credit on Excess over Amount in Column A (%) |
|---|---|---|---|
| 4,100,000 | 5,100,000 | 290,800 | 11.2 |
| 5,100,000 | 6,100,000 | 402,800 | 12.0 |
| 6,100,000 | 7,100,000 | 522,800 | 12.8 |
| 7,100,000 | 8,100,000 | 650,800 | 13.6 |
| 8,100,000 | 9,100,000 | 786,800 | 14.4 |
| 9,100,000 | 10,100,000 | 930,800 | 15.2 |
| 10,100,000 | — | 1,082,800 | 16.0 |

## INHERITANCE TAX

Inheritance tax is a tax imposed on *receipt* of property resultant from death. Inheritance tax is due from the person who receives the Testator's property and is usually withheld from the amount of the bequest prior to distribution. Inheritance tax rates vary from state to state and with the relationship of the beneficiary to the Testator. Inheritance tax is separate from, and additional to, federal credit estate tax and state estate tax.

State inheritance and estate taxes are assessed on real property, personal property, and intangible personal property. State taxes apply to real property located within the state. Similarly, personal property located within a state is taxed by that state. If a person has residences in more than one state, taxing jurisdiction for intangible personal property such as stocks, bonds, and notes is the same as that of the primary residence or domicile. The primary residence is the one occupied for more than six months a year. Other jurisdiction factors include voter registration, issuance of a driver's license, and location of active checking and bank accounts. If you maintain residences in more than one state, it is important to establish your domicile clearly; otherwise, the states involved may all attempt to impose estate and inheritance taxes, thereby causing additional delay and expense in settling your estate.

## GIFT TAX

Six states (Delaware, Louisiana, New York, North Carolina, Tennessee, and Wisconsin) also levy gift taxes. Generally, credit for gift taxes paid at the state level is handled in a similar manner as it is for federal gift taxes. Eighteen states, (refer to the State Summary, Chapter 9) have followed the federal lead and have included generation-skipping transfers when calculating estate tax liability. These states have referenced the federal regulations regarding definitions and reporting of generation-skipping transfers.

# *Insufficient Assets*

If your estate is not sufficient to pay all your debts, each state establishes the priority of claims against the estate. Generally, payment of expenses and debts is in the following order:

1. Court fees and costs.

2. Funeral, burial, or cremation expenses.

3. Estate administration costs, fees, and expenses (legal fees, personal representative compensation, and real estate brokerage commissions from sale of the estate's real property).

4. Spousal and family allowance.

5. Taxes.

6. Reasonable expenses for last illness (medical, hospital, nursing).

7. Last three months of rent in arrears.

8. Last three months of wages, salaries, or commissions due to be paid.

9. All other claims.

Given insufficient funds remaining after priorities 1–8 (above) have been paid, all claims listed under priority 9 must be paid proportionally. If all these costs have been paid, bequests will be honored in the following sequence:

1. Specific and monetary bequests.

2. A general (not source- or item-specific) bequest to the surviving spouse.

3. General bequest to others.

4. Residual bequest(s).

Clearly, if review of your estate reveals a potential shortfall, it is prudent to purchase life insurance in an amount sufficient to deal with the situation or to develop another contingency plan.

# CHAPTER 8

# The Living Will/ Durable Power of Attorney

## Introduction

The debate over the right to death with dignity has long been a subject of national concern and publicity. Only in recent years has the individual's right to declare, in advance, the type of medical treatment that can be used to prolong life been recognized as a fact of law. A properly signed and witnessed Living Will, advance medical directive, or Durable Power of Attorney allows you to state, in advance, your instructions regarding the use of life-sustaining measures in the event you suffer a terminal condition.

A discussion of Living Wills, advance medical directives, and the Durable Power of Attorney is included in this book because of the role these documents can play in estate planning. Decisions regarding medical care are entirely personal, and the importance of a Living Will is subjective with each individual. The information presented in this chapter should provide you with sufficient knowledge to make informed decisions concerning your personal situation. In this day of advanced medical technology, when physical life can be sustained far beyond the hope of recovery, the value of an advance medical directive is increasingly important.

All but a few states now recognize a statutory form of Living Will or other advance medical directive. Although these documents may have different formal titles, they all allow an individual to set out instructions to medical personnel regarding treatment in the event of a terminal illness or condition. In the interest of simplicity, these documents are referred to as the Living Will or advance medical directive in the following chapter. The Living Will, Directive to Physicians, DNR (Do Not Resuscitate) order, and other advance medical directives, no matter what they are called, achieve a similar purpose: They allow you to state beforehand the type of medical treatment you consent to have administered in the event you suffer a terminal illness. A Living Will is effective even if you become unconscious, comatose, or otherwise physically unable to communicate.

Keep in mind that a Living Will or other advance medical directive contains instructions for only doctors, nurses, or other medical personnel. You should also be aware that there are some differences in the types, and extent, of instructions that are allowed in different states. Because of these variations, it is important to obtain current information regarding advance medical directives in your state.

A Living Will may be revoked at any time, by a written revocation, destruction of the original document, or oral declaration.

If a Living Will or other advance medical directive is too restrictive, or does not meet your needs, you may consider a Durable Power of Attorney.

A Durable Power of Attorney (or Durable Power of Attorney for Health Care) is a legal document that allows you to appoint an agent to make medical decisions on your behalf. Your designated agent (Attorney-in-Fact) is empowered to instruct medical personnel about the treatment you have chosen in the event you suffer a terminal condition.

Remember, while a Durable Power of Attorney for Health Care empowers your agent to act for you in health care matters only, the regular Durable Power of Attorney offers more latitude in the types of instructions you may give. Your designated agent must agree to act on your behalf and carry out your orders, which, of course, must be legal and reasonable. Because a Durable Power of Attorney may contain instructions empowering your agent to act for you in business or other matters, it offers additional flexibility.

## Obtaining Current Information

Because laws and policies regarding Living Wills and other advance medical directives are fairly new, it is important to have current information as to requirements and the proper forms for your state. A reference guide to state, national, and private resources is included in this chapter for your convenience. You may contact these sources and organizations directly for information about state policies and procedures concerning Living Wills and other advance medical directives. Many of these sources can also supply forms that comply with statutes in your state. Your family doctor, attorney, medical facility, and many local organizations may also furnish current information about advance medical directives.

Decisions regarding life support should be considered carefully and discussed with your family, physician, and others who may be concerned. A Living Will or other advance medical directive can be effective only if it is properly prepared, the persons involved are fully informed, and it is available when needed. A sample of a generic Living Will appears as an illustration at the end of this chapter. Due to the differences in state forms, it is impractical to provide illustrations for every state.

# Reasons for a Living Will

Although purposes vary with the individual, the three primary reasons for preparing a Living Will or other advance directive are:

**1.** *To limit the use of artificial methods of prolonging life in the event of an irreversible terminal illness or condition.* Medical technology has advanced to the point that life may be sustained through a variety of methods, even when there is no reasonable hope that the patient will survive. A Living Will provides medical personnel with your instructions regarding the use of medical treatment to prolong life.

The artificial extension of life may cause extreme physical, emotional, and financial consequences. In some cases doctors may withhold pain-relieving medications in an attempt to prolong the life of terminal patients. Family resources and emotions may be stressed needlessly as a parent, child, spouse, or other close relative is maintained by artificial means.

A Living Will allows you to determine the treatment you wish to receive, even if you become physically or mentally incapable of communicating your wishes. A natural death is often felt to be preferable to the artificial extension of life through technology.

**2.** *To guard against the inability to communicate wishes regarding medical treatment because of illness, injuries, unconsciousness, or irrevocable brain damage.* A Living Will declares, in advance, the medical procedures that you consent to have administered in the event you become terminally ill or injured, even if you are unconscious, comatose, or physically unable to communicate. Without a Living Will or other advance medical directive, you may forfeit the ability to participate in decisions regarding treatment if you are unable to speak, signal, or otherwise communicate.

**3.** *To help protect personal and family assets from being exhausted by the high costs that may result from the extension of life by artificial means.* Advances in medical science have made it possible to maintain the basic life functions by artificial means for extensive periods of time. Respirators, intubation, and other techniques can replace, or augment, failing bodily functions.

These artificial life-support measures are expensive, and they may be used even when the patient has no hope of recovery. The cost of this type of treatment can place an extreme financial burden on personal and family assets. Your estate may be greatly reduced by the expense of such treatment. A Living Will lets you state the extent to which artificial means may be used to prolong life in the event you suffer a terminal illness or condition.

Although the individual reasons may differ, the effect of a Living Will or other advance medical directive in estate planning is obvious: A Living Will can help preserve estate assets that could otherwise be depleted by the expense of extreme medical measures. A Living Will or other advance medical directive can be an effective tool in planning, and preserving, your estate.

## The Growing Need for Advance Medical Directives

The need for a document like the Living Will has grown as people live longer and medical technology improves. In years past the majority of Americans were little concerned with the possibility of being kept artificially alive through medical means. The reason was simple: most died at home and the opportunity for such care was not widely available. This situation has changed dramatically in recent years. The majority of Americans now die while in the care of a medical or nursing institution. This significant change has made the need for a Living Will or other advance directive more crucial.

The primary reasons for this change are related. Americans now live longer, due in large measure to improvements in income, diet, medical care, and access to medical facilities. Medical science and technology have advanced rapidly, developing drugs, techniques, and machinery that can prolong life in emergency circumstances, but cannot prevent death in terminal situations. Even basic medical care facilities are often equipped with life-support technology that would have seemed futuristic 20 years ago. The use of such technology is very beneficial in many situations. Patients may be sustained artificially while awaiting transfer to better equipped medical facilities or, in some cases, while awaiting a medical specialist. Life-support equipment may be used while a transplant patient is awaiting a donor organ. In some circumstances doctors have used an induced coma as a medical technique in brain damage cases, with life-support equipment being used to stabilize and maintain a patient while the healing process takes place. For all the good this technology does, in some cases it can be used to prolong life unnecessarily.

Most people strongly support the use of medical technology to sustain life when the patient has a genuine chance for recovery, but the extensive use of medical technology to prolong life when there is little or no hope of recovery is a prospect that few would endorse. The Living Will, or other advance directive, can help prevent the use of extreme measures to prolong life when the patient has no chance of regaining the ability to survive independently.

## LEGAL CASES

There have been a number of nationally publicized legal cases concerning "right to die" issues that dramatically illustrate the need for a Living Will. The case of Karen Ann Quinlan is one many people remember, although it was in the news several years ago. A more recent case was influential in bringing about changes in laws and public education regarding advance medical directives.

The Cruzan case, which reached the U.S. Supreme Court in 1990, involved a young woman who was the victim of an automobile accident. The injuries sustained by Nancy Cruzan left her with irreversible brain damage—without the ability to survive independently and unable to communicate. After the comatose patient had been kept alive artificially in a vegetative state for seven years, her parents sought to have the hydration and feeding of their daughter terminated so that she could die peacefully. Citing state laws requiring proof of intent, the hospital refused to comply with the family's wishes.

Lower courts in the state of Missouri, where Nancy Cruzan was hospitalized, agreed with the parents and determined that there was enough evidence to strongly suggest that her decision, could she express it, would be to die with dignity. The Missouri Supreme Court, in a later reversal, found that state law required reliable and strong evidence that the victim wanted to end her life and held that, because she did not express it in advance and could not communicate, there was insufficient evidence of that intent in the Cruzan case.

The case of *Cruzan v. Director, Missouri Department of Health* then reached the U.S. Supreme Court. The Supreme Court's decision was significant in two ways. The Court affirmed clearly the constitutional right to reject unwanted medical treatment that prolongs life artificially—if that is the informed intent of the patient. However, in sending the case back to Missouri for adjudication, the Court also found that the states could enact reasonable rules of proof to establish the intent of the patient; in this case the patient could not speak or communicate, and therefore could not state her intent. (A Missouri state court later found that there was evidence of intent and complied with the family's wishes. Artificial hydration and feeding were discontinued and the patient was allowed to die peacefully.)

The Cruzan case dramatically illustrated the value of a Living Will, advance medical directive, or other method to establish the limits of medical care.

## THE PATIENT SELF-DETERMINATION ACT

Publicity surrounding the Cruzan case and a number of others, along with attendant public pressure, is partially responsible for the Patient Self-Determination Act, passed by Congress in 1990. This act requires health institutions to inform patients of their right to declare their wishes regarding medical treatment through a Living Will, other advance directive, or oral declaration.

Health care institutions are also required to develop policies regarding those directives. Almost all states have passed legislation conforming to the federal act or have had court decisions in concurrence. The result has been a greater public awareness of the Living Will and other options regarding medical care.

The Patient Self-Determination Act generally requires medical personnel to inform the patient, when entering the institution, of state laws and institutional policy regarding advance medical directives. A brief summary of the requirements follows.

**A.** You should be provided with a description of the applicable law, requirements, rights, and duties concerning advance directives or the instruction not to resuscitate. This description must state and define the rights you have regarding Do Not Resuscitate (DNR) orders, Living Wills, or other advance medical directives.

**B.** Your medical record must note that you have prepared a Living Will or other advance directive.

**C.** You should be provided with a statement that sets out the policy of the institution regarding the implementation of Do Not Resuscitate orders, advance directives, or Living Wills.

**D.** You may not be discriminated against because you have a Living Will, DNR order, or other advance directive.

**E.** To inform the public, the institution should provide staff and community education programs regarding the subject of advance directives. Education programs are required for providers participating in Medicaid and Medicare programs.

**F.** You should be informed about advance directives whether you are an inpatient or an outpatient.

The general purpose of the Patient Self-Determination Act is to require all health care institutions to have an active policy that informs patients of their rights regarding advance medical directives. Most states have now passed laws similar to the federal act. The Patient Self-Determination Act has resulted in greater public awareness of the options concerning medical treatment.

## Preparing an Advance Medical Directive

The Patient Self-Determination Act, state statutes concerning patients' rights, and education have made Americans more fully informed about their rights in regard to advance medical directives. Although all advance medical directives have a similar purpose, the actual language, scope, and requirements of proof differ from state to state. If you decide to execute a Living Will or advance directive you should be aware of current state requirements and obtain the proper forms.

Advance medical directive and/or Living Will forms and current information are available through a number of state, national, professional, and private organizations. Because of the differences in state laws it is important to obtain the correct form for your state. A list of sources that may provide appropriate forms is included in this chapter.

## STATE REQUIREMENTS

Although there are differences in state requirements and forms, the general requirements and procedures for executing a Living Will or advance medical directive are similar in all states. In simplest terms, to write a Living Will you must be an adult, be of sound mind, and be able to comprehend the nature of your acts. Although some states require only notarization, a Living Will is usually witnessed in a manner similar to a testamentary will.

Many states now have statutory forms for preparing a Living Will or other advance medical directive to instruct health care personnel about your decisions regarding life support and related medical treatment. A Living Will or other advance medical directive prepared in one state will usually be honored in another as long as state laws do not conflict.

## PLANNING STEPS

**1.** Consider your decision regarding advance medical directives carefully, and then discuss your plans with your family, doctor, attorney, or others concerned. It is important to have the support and agreement of those involved to assure that your directions regarding medical treatment are followed.

**2.** Get current information about the requirements and policies of your state. Many states have adopted laws and policies regarding advance medical directives, providing information and forms through state offices, medical facilities, and other private and public organizations. Be sure to review the state policies and requirements, and language contained on forms, to make sure that they meet your needs. If a statutory Living Will or other advance directive is too restrictive or does not meet your needs, you may wish to consider a Durable Power of Attorney.

**3.** Prepare your Living Will or other advance directive according to state requirements, making sure to have it properly witnessed or notarized. Be sure you notify those who are involved; your doctor, family, and others concerned should be fully informed.

## Durable Power of Attorney

The Durable Power of Attorney is a legal document that may be used to direct the limits, and type, of medical treatment. A Durable Power of Attorney allows you to authorize an agent (Attorney-in-Fact) to make medical decisions on your behalf, even if you become incapacitated.

You may specify exactly what your Attorney-in-Fact is empowered to decide on your behalf. You may set out specific directions regarding the use of medical measures to sustain life, and the decisions your agent can make for you. A Durable Power of Attorney may also contain a variety of other provisions regarding decisions your agent is empowered to make on your behalf in addition to health care matters.

A Durable Power of Attorney can empower your agent to make decisions regarding minor children or other dependents. You may also empower your agent to make business and financial decisions, such as settling real estate matters on your behalf. A Durable Power of Attorney can contain more extensive and detailed directions than a Living Will, which is typically directed only to physicians or medical personnel.

If you prepare a Durable Power of Attorney, you must be sure the agent you name to carry out your directions agrees to do so. You should consult with the person you choose to be your agent and make sure that he or she agrees to be appointed and carry out your directions. Because of the far-reaching legal implications, the differences in state laws, and the broad powers that can be conveyed to your agent, it is usually advisable to seek professional assistance when preparing a Durable Power of Attorney.

# *Resources*

The following list of public and private institutions and organizations can provide current information regarding Living Wills and other advance medical directives. A state-by-state guide to legal resources is included so that you may obtain current information concerning your state. In addition to these resources, most state health agencies, medical institutions, and a wide variety of other organizations now provide information about advance medical directives.

American Association of Retired Persons
Free brochure, "Shaping Your Health Care Future with Health
   Care Advance Directives," available; request stock # D-15-803 from:
AARP Fulfillment
601 E Street NW
Washington, DC 20049

AARP Legal Counsel for the Elderly
1909 K Street NW
Washington, DC 20049
Telephone: 202-833-6720

American Bar Association
1800 M Street NW, South Lobby
Washington, DC 20036
Telephone: 202-331-2200

Choice in Dying, Inc.
200 Varick Street, 10th Floor
New York, NY 10014-4810
Telephone: 212-366-5540

## ALABAMA

Attorney General

State House

11 South Union Street

Montgomery, AL 36101

334-242-7300

State Bar Association

Post Office Box 671

Montgomery, AL 36101

334-269-1515

800-392-5660 (in state)

## ALASKA

Attorney General

State Capitol

Post Office Box 110300

Juneau, AK 99811-0300

907-465-3600

State Bar Association

Post Office Box 100279

Anchorage, AK 99511

907-272-0352

## ARIZONA

Attorney General

1275 West Washington

Phoenix, AZ 85007

602-542-4266

State Bar of Arizona

111 West Monroe

Phoenix, AZ 85003

602-252-4804

## ARKANSAS

Attorney General

200 Tower Building

323 Center Street

Little Rock, AR 72201-2610

501-682-2007

State Bar Association

400 West Markham Street

Little Rock, AR 72201

501-375-4605

## CALIFORNIA

Attorney General

1300 I Street

Sacramento, CA 95814

916-324-5437

State Bar of California

555 Franklin Street

San Francisco, CA 94102

415-561-8200

## COLORADO

Attorney General

Department of Law

1525 Sherman Street

Denver, CO 80203

303-866-3611

State Bar Association

1900 Grant Street

Suite 950

Denver, CO 80203

303-860-1115

## CONNECTICUT

Attorney General

55 Elm Street

Hartford, CT 06106

203-566-2026

State Bar Association

101 Corporate Place

Rocky Hill, CT 06067-1894

203-721-0025

## DELAWARE

Attorney General

820 North French Street, 8th Floor

Wilmington, DE 19801

302-577-3838

State Bar Association

1201 Orange Street

Wilmington, DE 19801

302-658-5279

## DISTRICT OF COLUMBIA

Office of the Attorney General

555 4th Street, NW

Washington, DC 20001

202-514-6600

District of Columbia Bar

1250 H Street, NW

Washington, DC 20005

202-737-4700

## FLORIDA

Attorney General

State Capitol, PL 01

Tallahassee, FL 32399-1050

904-487-1963

State Bar Association

650 Appalachia Parkway

Tallahassee, FL 32399-2300

904-561-5600

## GEORGIA

Attorney General

40 Capitol Square, SW

Atlanta, GA 30334-1300

404-656-4585

State Bar of Georgia

800 The Hurt Building

50 Hurt Plaza

Atlanta, GA 30303

404-527-8700

## GUAM

Attorney General

Department of Law

238 O'Hara Street

Agana, Guam 96910

671-472-6841

## HAWAII

Attorney General

425 Queen Street

Honolulu, HI 96813

808-586-1282

State Bar Association

1136 Union Mall

Honolulu, HI 96813

808-537-1868

## IDAHO

Attorney General

Post Office Box 83720

Boise, ID 83720

208-334-2400

State Bar Association

525 West Jefferson Street

Boise, ID 83701

208-334-4500

## ILLINOIS

Attorney General

500 South 2nd Street

Springfield, IL 62706

217-782-1090

State Bar Association

424 South 2nd Street

Springfield, IL 62706

217-525-1760

## INDIANA

Attorney General

402 West Washington Street

Indianapolis, IN 46204

317-232-6201

State Bar Association

230 East Ohio Street, 4th Floor

Indianapolis, IN 46204

317-639-5465

## IOWA

Attorney General

Hoover Building, 2nd Floor

Des Moines, IA 50319

515-281-5164

State Bar Association

Suite 300

521 East Locust Street

Des Moines, IA 50309-1939

515-243-3179

## KANSAS

Attorney General

301 West 10th Avenue

Topeka, KS 66612-1579

913-296-2215

State Bar Association

1200 S.W. Harrison

Topeka, KS 66601

913-234-5696

## KENTUCKY

Attorney General

Post Office Box 2000

700 Capitol Avenue

Frankfort, KY 40602

502-564-7600

State Bar Association

514 West Main Street

Frankfort, KY 40601

502-564-3795

## LOUISIANA

Attorney General

301 Main Street

Baton Rouge, LA 70801

504-342-7013

State Bar Association

601 St. Charles Avenue

New Orleans, LA 70130

504-566-1600

## MAINE

Attorney General

State House; Station #6

Augusta, ME 04333

207-626-8800

State Bar Association

124 State Street; P.O. Box 788

Augusta, ME 04332

207-622-7523

## MARYLAND

Attorney General

200 St. Paul Place

Baltimore, MD 21202

410-576-6300

State Bar Association

520 West Sayette Street

Baltimore, MD 21201

410-685-7878

## MASSACHUSETTS

Attorney General

One Ashburton Place

Boston, MA 02108

617-727-2200

State Bar Association

20 West Street

Boston, MA 02111

617-542-3602

## MICHIGAN

Attorney General

Law Building; P.O. Box 30212

525 West Ottawa Street

Lansing, MI 48909

517-373-1110

State Bar of Michigan

306 Townsend Street

Lansing, MI 48933

517-372-9030

## MINNESOTA

Attorney General

102 State Capitol

St. Paul, MN 55155

612-296-6196

State Bar Association

514 Nicollet Mall, Suite 300

Minneapolis, MN 55402

612-333-1183

## MISSISSIPPI

Attorney General

Gartin Justice Building; P.O. Box 220

Jackson, MS 39205

601-359-3680

State Bar Association

Post Office Box 2168

Jackson, MS 39225-2168

601-948-4471

## MISSOURI

Attorney General

Post Office Box 899

Jefferson City, MO 65102

314-751-3321

The Missouri Bar Association

326 Monroe Street

Jefferson City, MO 65101

314-635-4128

## MONTANA

Attorney General

Justice Building

215 North Sanders

Helena, MT 59620

406-444-2026

State Bar of Montana

Post Office Box 577

Helena, MT 59624

406-442-7660

## NEBRASKA

Attorney General

2115 State Capitol; P.O. Box 89820

Lincoln, NE 68509

402-471-2682

State Bar Association

635 South 14th Street

Lincoln, NE 68501

402-475-7091

## NEVADA

Attorney General

Capitol Complex

198 South Carson Street

Carson City, NV 89710

702-687-4170

State Bar Association

1325 Airmotive Way

Reno, NV 89502

702-329-4100

## NEW HAMPSHIRE

Attorney General

33 Capitol Street

Concord, NH 03301-6397

603-271-3658

State Bar Association

112 Pleasant Street

Concord, NH 03301

603-224-6942

## NEW JERSEY

Attorney General

CN 080

Trenton, NJ 08625

609-292-4925

State Bar Association

1 Newark Center, 16th Floor

Newark, NJ 07102-5268

201-622-6207

## NEW MEXICO

Attorney General

407 Galisteo Street, Room 260

Post Office Box 1508

Santa Fe, NM 87504-1508

505-827-6000

State Bar of New Mexico

Post Office Box 25883

Albuquerque, NM 87125

505-842-6132

## NEW YORK

Attorney General

State Capitol

Albany, NY 12224

518-474-7330

State Bar Association

One Elk Street

Albany, NY 12207

518-463-3200

## NORTH CAROLINA

Attorney General

Department of Justice

Post Office Box 629

Raleigh, NC 27602-0629

919-733-3377

State Bar Association

Post Office Box 25908

Raleigh, NC 27611

919-828-4620

## NORTH DAKOTA

Attorney General

State Capitol

600 East Boulevard Avenue

Bismarck, ND 58505-0040

701-328-2218

State Bar Association

600 East Boulevard Avenue

Bismarck, ND 58505-0530

701-328-4201

## OHIO

Attorney General

State Office Tower

30 East Broad Street

Columbus, OH 43266-0410

614-466-3376

State Bar Association

1700 Lake Shore Drive

Post Office Box 6562

Columbus, OH 43216-6562

614-487-2050

## OKLAHOMA

Attorney General

2300 North Lincoln Boulevard, Room 112

Oklahoma City, OK 73105

405-521-3921

State Bar Association

Post Office Box 53036

Oklahoma City, OK 73152

405-524-2365

## OREGON

Attorney General

100 Justice Building

1162 Court Street, NE

Salem, OR 97310

503-378-6002

State Bar Association

Post Office Box 1689

Lake Oswego, OR 97035

503-620-0222

800-452-8260 (in state)

## PENNSYLVANIA

Attorney General

Strawberry Square, 16th Floor

Harrisburg, PA 17120

717-787-3391

State Bar Association

100 South Street; P.O. Box 186

Harrisburg, PA 17108

717-238-6715

## PUERTO RICO

Court Administration

Post Office Box 190917

San Juan, PR 00919-0917

809-763-3049

State Bar Association

Post Office Box 190917

San Juan, PR 00919-0917

809-724-3358

## RHODE ISLAND

Attorney General

72 Pine Street

Providence, RI 02903

401-274-4400

State Bar Association

115 Cedar Street

Providence, RI 02903

401-421-5740

## SOUTH CAROLINA

Attorney General

R.C.D. Office Building

P.O. Box 11549

Columbia, SC 29211

803-734-3970

South Carolina State Bar

Post Office Box 608

Columbia, SC 29202-0608

803-799-6653

## SOUTH DAKOTA

Attorney General

500 East Capitol Avenue

Pierre, SD 57501

605-773-3215

State Bar of South Dakota

222 East Capitol Avenue

Pierre, SD 57501

605-224-7554

## TENNESSEE

| Attorney General | State Bar Association |
| --- | --- |
| 450 James Robertson Parkway | 3622 West End Avenue |
| Nashville, TN 37243-0485 | Nashville, TN 37205 |
| 615-741-3491 | 615-383-7421 |

## TEXAS

| Attorney General | State Bar of Texas |
| --- | --- |
| Post Office Box 12548 | Post Office Box 12487 |
| Austin, TX 78711-2548 | Austin, TX 78711 |
| 512-463-2191 | 512-463-1463 |

## UTAH

| Attorney General | State Bar Association |
| --- | --- |
| 236 State Capitol | 645 South 200 East Street |
| Salt Lake City, UT 84114 | Salt Lake City, UT 84111 |
| 801-538-1015 | 801-531-9110 |

## VERMONT

| Attorney General | State Bar Association |
| --- | --- |
| 109 State Street | Post Office Box 100 |
| Montpelier, VT 05609-1001 | Montpelier, VT 05601 |
| 802-828-3171 | 802-223-2020 |

## VIRGINIA

| Attorney General | State Bar Association |
| --- | --- |
| 900 East Main Street, 6th Floor | 707 East Main Street, Suite 1500 |
| Richmond, VA 23219 | Richmond, VA 23219-2803 |
| 804-786-2071 | 804-775-0500 |

## WASHINGTON

Attorney General

1125 Washington Street, SE

Olympia, WA 98504-0100

360-753-6200

State Bar Association

2001 6th Avenue, Suite 500

Seattle, WA 98121

206-727-8200

## WEST VIRGINIA

Attorney General

1900 Kanawha Boulevard E

State Capitol; Building 1, Room E-26

Charleston, WV 25305

304-558-2021

State Bar Association

2006 Kanawha Boulevard E

Charleston, WV 25311

304-558-2456

## WISCONSIN

Attorney General

Post Office Box 7857

Madison, WI 53707-7857

608-266-1221

State Bar Association

Post Office Box 7158

Madison, WI 53707

608-257-3838

## WYOMING

Attorney General

123 State Capitol

Cheyenne, WY 82002

307-777-7841

State Bar Association

Post Office Box 109

Cheyenne, WY 82003

307-632-9061

# A LIVING WILL
# A DIRECTIVE TO PHYSICIANS

If I should have an incurable, terminal or irreversible condition that will cause my death within a relatively short time, it is my desire that my life not be prolonged by administration of life-sustaining procedures. If my condition is terminal and I am unable to participate in decisions regarding my medical treatment, I direct my attending physician to withhold or withdraw procedures that merely prolong the dying process and are not necessary to my comfort or freedom from pain. It is my intention that this declaration shall be valid until revoked by me.

Signed this _____ day of _____

Signature _____

City, County, and State of Residence _____

_____

The declarant is know to me and voluntarily signed this document in my presence.

Witness _____

Address _____

Witness _____

Address _____

County of _____

State of _____

Before me, the undersigned authority, personally appeared _____

_____, and _____ known to me to be Declarant and the witnesses whose names are signed to the foregoing instrument, and who, in the presence of each other, did subscribe their names to the Declaration on this date.

My commission expires:

[Seal]

_____
Notary Public

# CHAPTER 9

# State Summary

Any citizen of the United States who is at least 19 years old and is of sound mind may write his or her own will. A will written entirely by hand by the Testator is known as a holographic will. In most cases, a holographic will does not need to be witnessed; however, it must be properly constructed and the handwriting verified (proven) as that of the Testator. A testamentary will is a will that is signed and dated before witnesses. The advantage of the testamentary will is that it can be much more readily "proven" as the will of the Testator. Consequently, if you now have a holographic will, we strongly recommend that you revoke it by a new testamentary will.

## Summary of State Requirements

The requirements for writing a valid testamentary will are generally similar in all states and the District of Columbia. Differences in state requirements are summarized on pages 122 through 127.

*WITNESSES.* A testamentary will should be witnessed by "disinterested" persons, that is, people who are not mentioned in your will and who are not related to you. Louisiana and Vermont require three witnesses; the balance of the states require two witnesses to sign a will. If you own property in Vermont or Louisiana, it is advisable to have three witnesses. Your witnesses should also list their residential addresses next to their signatures.

*SELF-PROVING.* A self-proving certificate may be used to free witnesses from having to verify their signatures when the will is presented for probate. Self-proving is a convenience for your witnesses and can speed the probate process. Self-proving a will is optional but worth the brief additional time.

*COMMUNITY PROPERTY.* There are nine community-property states: Arizona, California, Idaho, Louisiana, Nevada, New Mexico, Texas, Washington, and Wisconsin. In a community-property state, all property owned by a mar-

## State Summary

| State | Court Having Probate Jurisdiction | Holographic Wills Recognized | Number of Witnesses | Self-Proving Recognized |
|---|---|---|---|---|
| **Alabama** | Probate Court | No | 2 | Yes |
| **Alaska** | Superior Court | Yes | 2 | Yes |
| **Arizona*** | Superior Court | Yes | 2 | Yes |
| **Arkansas** | Probate Court | Yes | 2 | Yes |
| **California*** | Superior Court | Yes | 2 | Yes |
| **Colorado** | District Court (Denver: Probate Court) | Yes | 2 | Yes |
| **Connecticut** | Probate Court | No | 2 | Yes |
| **Delaware** | Court of Chancery | No | 2 | Yes |
| **District of Columbia (DC)** | Superior Court | No | 2 | Yes |
| **Florida** | Circuit Court | No | 2 | Yes |
| **Georgia** | Probate Court | No | 2 | Yes |
| **Hawaii** | Circuit Court | No | 2 | Yes |
| **Idaho*** | District Court | Yes | 2 | Yes |
| **Illinois** | Circuit Court | No | 2 | No |
| **Indiana** | Circuit or Superior Court (Vigo and St. Joseph Counties: Probate Court) | No | 2 | Yes |
| **Iowa** | District Court | Yes | 2 | Yes |

*Community-property state.

ried couple is owned in one-half interest by each spouse. Exceptions include separate property brought into the marriage, property covered by valid prenuptial agreements, and property received through inheritance. Since community property does not include any right of survivorship, it is especially important to convey community-property interests with a valid will.

***NONRESIDENT EXECUTOR.*** All states allow a nonresident to act as Executor, most with no restrictions. Some states allow only close family members or primary beneficiaries to act as a nonresident Executor. Additionally, some states require that a nonresident Executor have a state resident act as a personal agent and post a surety bond.

***STATE TAXES.*** All states impose federal credit estate taxes, and many impose one or more of the following: estate tax, gift tax, generation-skipping transfer tax, and/or inheritance tax. Review the following State Summary for your state to identify applicable state taxes.

| Living Will Recognized | Taxes | | | | |
| --- | --- | --- | --- | --- | --- |
| | Federal Credit Estate | Estate | Gift | Generation- Skip Transfer | Inheritance |
| Yes | Yes | No | No | No | No |
| Yes | Yes | No | No | No | No |
| Yes | Yes | No | No | Yes | No |
| Yes | Yes | No | No | No | No |
| Yes | Yes | No | No | Yes | No |
| Yes | Yes | No | No | Yes | No |
| Yes | Yes | No | No | No | Yes |
| Yes | Yes | No | Yes | No | Yes |
| Yes | Yes | No | No | No | No |
| Yes | Yes | No | No | Yes | No |
| Yes | Yes | No | No | No | No |
| Yes | Yes | No | No | No | No |
| Yes | Yes | No | No | Yes | No |
| Yes | Yes | No | No | No | No |
| Yes | Yes | No | No | No | Yes |
| Yes | Yes | No | No | Yes | Yes |

*(continued)*

| State | Court Having Probate Jurisdiction | Holographic Wills Recognized | Number of Witnesses | Self-Proving Recognized |
|---|---|---|---|---|
| **Kansas** | District Court | No | 2 | Yes |
| **Kentucky** | District Court | Yes | 2 | Yes |
| **Louisiana*** | District Court | Yes | 3 3/5/7 | Yes |
| **Maine** | Probate Court | Yes | 2 | Yes |
| **Maryland** | Orphan's Court (Hartford and Montgomery Counties: Circuit Court) | Military (1 yr.) | 2 | Yes |
| **Massachusetts** | Probate and Family Court | No | 2 | Yes |
| **Michigan** | Probate Court | Yes | 2 | Yes |
| **Minnesota** | Probate Court | No | 2 | Yes |
| **Mississippi** | Chancery Court | Yes | 2 | Yes |
| **Missouri** | Circuit Court | No | 2 | Yes |
| **Montana** | District Court | Yes | 2 | Yes |
| **Nebraska** | County Court | Yes | 2 | Yes |
| **Nevada*** | District Court | Yes | 2 | Yes |
| **New Hampshire** | Probate Court | No | 2 | Yes |
| **New Jersey** | Surrogate's Court | Yes | 2 | Yes |
| **New Mexico*** | Probate or District Court | No | 2 | Yes |
| **New York** | Surrogate's Court | Military (War) | 2 | Yes |
| **North Carolina** | Superior Court | Yes | 2 | Yes |
| **North Dakota** | County Court | Yes | 2 | Yes |
| **Ohio** | Court of Common Pleas | No | 2 | Yes |
| **Oklahoma** | District Court | Yes | 2 | Yes |
| **Oregon** | Circuit or County Court | No | 2 | Yes |
| **Pennsylvania** | Common Pleas Court | Yes | 2 | Yes |
| **Rhode Island** | Probate Court | Yes | 2 | Yes |
| **South Carolina** | Probate Court | No | 2 | Yes |
| **South Dakota** | Circuit Court | Yes | 2 | Yes |
| **Tennessee** | Chancery Court (Davidson and Shelby Counties: Probate Court) | Yes | 2 | Yes |

*Community-property state.

| Living Will Recognized | Taxes | | | | |
| | Federal Credit Estate | Estate | Gift | Generation-Skip Transfer | Inheritance |
| --- | --- | --- | --- | --- | --- |
| Yes | Yes | No | No | Yes | Yes |
| Yes | Yes | No | No | No | Yes |
| Yes | Yes | No | Yes | No | Yes |
| Yes | Yes | No | No | No | No |
| Yes | Yes | No | No | No | Yes |
| No | Yes | Yes | No | Yes | Yes |
| Yes | Yes | No | No | Yes | Yes |
| Yes | Yes | No | No | No | No |
| Yes | Yes | Yes | No | No | No |
| Yes | Yes | No | No | Yes | No |
| Yes | Yes | No | No | No | Yes |
| Yes | Yes | No | No | No | Yes |
| Yes | Yes | No | No | Yes | No |
| Yes | Yes | No | No | No | Yes |
| Yes | Yes | No | No | No | Yes |
| Yes | Yes | No | No | No | No |
| No | Yes | Yes | Yes | No | No |
| Yes | Yes | No | Yes | Yes | Yes |
| Yes | Yes | No | No | No | No |
| No | Yes | Yes | No | Yes | No |
| Yes | Yes | Yes | No | No | No |
| Yes | Yes | No | No | No | No |
| No | Yes | No | No | No | Yes |
| No | Yes | Yes | No | Yes | No |
| Yes | Yes | Yes | No | Yes | No |
| No | Yes | No | No | No | Yes |
| Yes | Yes | No | Yes | Yes | Yes |

*(continued)*

## State Summary (continued)

| State | Court Having Probate Jurisdiction | Holographic Wills Recognized | Number of Witnesses | Self-Proving Recognized |
|---|---|---|---|---|
| **Texas*** | County or Probate Court | Yes | 2 | Yes |
| **Utah** | District Court | Yes | 2 | Yes |
| **Vermont** | Probate Court | No | 3 | No |
| **Virginia** | Circuit Court | Yes | 2 | Yes |
| **Washington*** | Superior Court | No | 2 | Yes |
| **West Virginia** | County Commissioner | Yes | 2 | No |
| **Wisconsin*** | Circuit Court | No | 2 | Yes |
| **Wyoming** | District Court | No | 2 | Yes |

*Community-property state.

# Intestate Succession

All states have laws of succession governing the distribution of the estates of their residents who die without a valid will (intestate). The laws of intestate succession are necessarily rather complex, since they cover every possible combination of potential heirs that might survive the decedent. According to the American Bar Association, over 70 percent of Americans die without exercising their right to prepare a valid will. Whenever this is the case, the estate must be distributed in accord with laws of succession of the state of the decedent's domicile.

Although it is assumed that the readers of this book recognize the importance and value of having a current, valid will, it is also clear that other adult family members or friends may not have a similar understanding. They may feel that the state's distribution formula will be in accord with their wishes and that a will is therefore unnecessary. For example, it is a common misconception that if there are no children of the marriage, the surviving spouse will inherit the entire estate. Although this happens in 20 states, it does *not* happen in the other 30 and in the District of Columbia. If the decedent had children, distribution becomes even more complex, varying according to whether the children are offspring of the marriage and how many children there are. Further, if there were children who have died, then their intestate shares pass to their children (if any) *per stirpes*.

Unless all adult members of your family have a valid will, you may well need to petition the local probate court to be appointed as Administrator of a relative's estate at some time in the future. A brief summary of state intestate succession basics is presented on the following pages. This summary material may assist you in understanding the gross estate distribution and perhaps, more importantly, help you convince loved ones of their need for a valid will.

| Living Will Recognized | Taxes | | | | |
| --- | --- | --- | --- | --- | --- |
| | Federal Credit Estate | Estate | Gift | Generation-Skip Transfer | Inheritance |
| Yes | Yes | No | No | Yes | Yes |
| Yes | Yes | No | No | No | No |
| Yes | Yes | No | No | No | No |
| Yes | Yes | No | No | Yes | No |
| Yes | Yes | No | No | No | No |
| Yes | Yes | No | No | No | No |
| Yes | Yes | No | Yes | No | No |
| Yes | Yes | No | No | No | No |

## ELECTIVE SHARE

All states allow a surviving spouse to elect to receive a share of his or her spouse's estate rather than the bequests contained in the will. This elective, or "forced," share is an outgrowth of dower and curtesy rights and is intended to protect the surviving spouse against total disinheritance. The elective share is generally a portion of the probate estate, although some states have expanded the assets covered to all property of the decedent, known as the "augmented estate." A petition for an elective share must be filed early in the probate process, usually within the first 60 days. The elective share is equal to, or, more frequently, less than, the spousal share under intestate succession. Often, no marital deduction can be taken for state estate and inheritance tax purposes if an elective share is received. The elective share varies from state to state and recently has been subject to more frequent legislative changes. If you are considering petitioning for an elective share, be sure to contact the local probate court to ascertain the actual amount that would be available at the time.

## SPOUSAL SHARE

The state intestate succession summary tables on pages 129 through 133 show the share that the surviving spouse would receive, which varies depending on the existence and number of other living potential heirs. These potential heirs are classified under five headings:

1. Children of the marriage (*per stirpes*).
2. Other children of the deceased spouse (*per stirpes*), which includes children from previous marriage(s) and illegitimate children.
3. No children but living parents of the deceased spouse.

4. No children and no living parents but brother(s) and/or sister(s) (*per stirpes*) of the deceased spouse.

5. No children, no living parents, and no brother(s) and/or sister(s).

In most states, in the last category (no children, no parents, and no brother(s) and/or sister(s) of the deceased spouse), the surviving spouse will inherit the entire estate. However, in Arkansas, Maine, Massachusetts, Oklahoma, Rhode Island, South Carolina, Texas, Vermont, and the District of Columbia, the surviving spouse will receive the entire estate only if there are also no living grandparents and no living descendants of the deceased spouse's grandparents as well.

Other special cases occur in Georgia, Mississippi, and Oklahoma, which provide for the spouse and children to receive equal shares, which means that the more children there are, the smaller the surviving spouse's share becomes. Arkansas requires the spouse to have been married for three years to obtain the full intestate succession share; otherwise, the share is diminished proportionally. Although not a community-property state, Oklahoma treats property gained during the marriage separately from other property. Louisiana, a community-property state, grants the surviving spouse a life estate interest in real property as long as the surviving spouse does not remarry, whereas Tennessee grants homestead and a one-year living allowance to the surviving spouse, not to be less than one-third of the estate. As you review this information, you will see how important having a valid will is to all your loved ones.

## COMMUNITY-PROPERTY STATES

There are two types of property in community-property states: community property and separate property. Community property is all property owned by the couple during their marriage, and each has a one-half interest in it. Separate property is property owned solely by one spouse, such as an inheritance or assets identified in a valid prenuptial agreement. These two types of property are treated differently under intestate succession in all community-property states except Wisconsin.

## LIFE ESTATE

A life estate is an interest in, and right to use, real property for the lifetime of the life estate holder. It is not ownership but rather a terminable interest. Six states and the District of Columbia grant life estate interests in real property to the surviving spouse under intestate succession. Louisiana (listed previously under community-property states) also grants spousal life estate interest if the surviving spouse does not remarry.

## Surviving Spouse Share in Community-Property States

| State | If Deceased Had Children | | If Deceased Had No Children, and There Are | | |
|---|---|---|---|---|---|
| | Children of Marriage Only | Other Children of Deceased | Living Parents of Deceased | No Living Parents but Living Siblings of Deceased | No Living Parents or Siblings of Deceased |
| | Then the Surviving Spouse Receives | | | | |
| **Arizona** | | | | | |
| Community | $1/2$ | None | All | All | All |
| Separate | All | $1/2$ | All | All | All |
| **California** | | | | | |
| Community | All | All | All | All | All |
| Separate | | | $1/2$ | $1/2$ | All |
| 1 child | $1/2$ | $1/2$ | | | |
| 2 or more | $1/3$ | $1/3$ | | | |
| **Idaho** | | | | | |
| Community | All | All | All | All | All |
| Separate | $50,000 + 1/2$ | $1/2$ | $50,000 + 1/2$ | All | All |
| **Louisiana** | | | | | |
| Community | Life estate if no remarriage | | All | All | All |
| Separate | None | None | None | None | All |
| **Nevada** | | | | | |
| Community | All | All | All | All | All |
| Separate | | | $1/2$ | $1/2$ | All |
| 1 child | $1/2$ | $1/2$ | | | |
| 2 or more | $1/3$ | $1/3$ | | | |
| **New Mexico** | | | | | |
| Community | All | All | All | All | All |
| Separate | $1/4$ | $1/4$ | All | All | All |
| **Texas** | | | | | |
| Community | $1/2$ | $1/2$ | All | All | All |
| Separate | $1/3$ | $1/3$ | $1/2$ | $1/2$ | All* |
| **Washington** | | | | | |
| Community | All | All | All | All | All |
| Separate | $1/2$ | $1/3$ | $3/4$ | $3/4$ | All |
| **Wisconsin** | | | | | |
| Community | All | $1/2$ | All | All | All |
| Separate | All | $1/2$ | All | All | All |

*If no living grandparents and no living descendants of deceased spouse's grandparents; otherwise, same as previous category.

## *Surviving Spouse Share in States with Life Estate Interests*

| State | If Deceased Had Children | | If Deceased Had No Children, and There Are | | |
| --- | --- | --- | --- | --- | --- |
| | Children of Marriage Only | Other Children of Deceased | Living Parents of Deceased | No Living Parents but Living Siblings of Deceased | No Living Parents or Siblings of Deceased |
| | | | Then the Surviving Spouse Receives | | |
| **Arkansas** | | | | | |
| Real property | Life estate + $1/3$ | Life estate + $1/3$ | All* | All* | All* |
| Personal property | $1/3$ | $1/3$ | All* | All* | All* |
| **Delaware** | | | | | |
| Real property | Life estate | Life estate | Life estate | Life estate | All |
| Personal property | $5,000 + $1/2$ | $1/2$ | $50,000 + $1/2$ | All | All |
| **District of Columbia** | | | | | |
| Real property | Life estate + $1/3$ | Life estate | Life estate + $1/3$ | Life estate + $1/3$ | All |
| Personal property | $1/3$ | $1/3$ | $1/2$ | $1/2$ | All** |
| **Indiana** | | | | | |
| Real property | Life estate | Life estate | $3/4$ | All | All |
| Personal property | | | $3/4$ | All | All |
| 1 child | $1/2$ | $1/2$ | | | |
| 2 or more | $1/3$ | $1/3$ | | | |
| **Kentucky** | | | | | |
| Real property | Life estate + $1/3$ | Life estate + $1/3$ | $1/2$ | $1/2$ | All |
| Personal property | $1/2$ | $1/2$ | $1/2$ | $1/2$ | All |
| **Rhode Island** | | | | | |
| Real property | Life estate | Life estate | Life estate + $75,000 | Life estate + $75,000 | All** |
| Personal property | $1/2$ | $1/2$ | $50,000 + $1/2$ | $50,000 + $1/2$ | All** |
| **West Virginia** | | | | | |
| Real property | $1/3$ | Life estate | All | All | All |
| Personal property | $1/3$ | $1/3$ | All | All | All |

*If married 3 years; otherwise $1/2$.

**If no living grandparents and no living descendants of deceased spouse's grandparents; otherwise, same as previous category.

## Surviving Spouse Share in All Other States

| State | If Deceased Had Children | | If Deceased Had No Children, and There Are | | |
| | Children of Marriage Only | Other Children of Deceased | Living Parents of Deceased | No Living Parents but Living Siblings of Deceased | No Living Parents or Siblings of Deceased |
|---|---|---|---|---|---|
| | Then the Surviving Spouse Receives | | | | |
| **Alabama** | $50,000 + $\frac{1}{2}$ | $\frac{1}{2}$ | $100,000 + $\frac{1}{2}$ | All | All |
| **Alaska** | $50,000 + $\frac{1}{2}$ | $\frac{1}{2}$ | $5,000 + $\frac{1}{2}$ | All | All |
| **Colorado** | $25,000 + $\frac{1}{2}$ | $\frac{1}{2}$ | All | All | All |
| **Connecticut** | $100,000 + $\frac{1}{2}$ | $\frac{1}{2}$ | $100,000 + $\frac{3}{4}$ | All | All |
| **Florida** | $20,000 + $\frac{1}{2}$ | $\frac{1}{2}$ | All | All | All |
| **Georgia** | Equal shares with children (spouse $\frac{1}{4}$ minimum) | | All | All | All |
| **Hawaii** | $\frac{1}{2}$ | $\frac{1}{2}$ | $\frac{1}{2}$ | All | All |
| **Illinois** | $\frac{1}{2}$ | $\frac{1}{2}$ | All | All | All |
| **Iowa** | All | $\frac{1}{2}$ (Not less than $50,000) | All | All | All |
| **Kansas** | $\frac{1}{2}$ | $\frac{1}{2}$ | All | All | All |
| **Maine** | $50,000 + $\frac{1}{2}$ | $\frac{1}{2}$ | $50,000 + $\frac{1}{2}$ | $50,000 + $\frac{1}{2}$ | All* |
| **Maryland** Minor child | $15,000 + $\frac{1}{2}$ <br> $\frac{1}{2}$ | $15,000 + $\frac{1}{2}$ <br> $\frac{1}{2}$ | $15,000 + $\frac{1}{2}$ | All | All |
| **Massachusetts** | $\frac{1}{2}$ | $\frac{1}{2}$ | $200,000 + $\frac{1}{2}$ | $200,000 + $\frac{1}{2}$ | All |
| **Michigan** | $60,000 + $\frac{1}{2}$ | $\frac{1}{2}$ | $60,000 + $\frac{1}{2}$ | All | All |
| **Minnesota** | $70,000 + $\frac{1}{2}$ | $\frac{1}{2}$ | All | All | All |
| **Mississippi** | Equal shares with children | | All | All | All |
| **Missouri** | $20,000 + $\frac{1}{2}$ | $\frac{1}{2}$ | $20,000 + $\frac{1}{2}$ | All | All |
| **Montana** | | | All | All | All |
| 1 child | All | $\frac{1}{2}$ | | | |
| 2 or more | All | $\frac{1}{3}$ | | | |

*If married 3 years; otherwise $\frac{1}{2}$.

**If no living grandparents and no living descendants of deceased spouse's grandparents; otherwise, same as previous category.

*(continued)*

| State | If Deceased Had Children | | If Deceased Had No Children, and There Are | | |
| | Children of Marriage Only | Other Children of Deceased | Living Parents of Deceased | No Living Parents but Living Siblings of Deceased | No Living Parents or Siblings of Deceased |
|---|---|---|---|---|---|
| | | Then the Surviving Spouse Receives | | | |
| **Nebraska** | $50,000 + $\frac{1}{2}$ | $\frac{1}{2}$ | $50,000 + $\frac{1}{2}$ | All | All |
| **New Hampshire** | $50,000 + $\frac{1}{2}$ | $\frac{1}{3}$ | $50,000 + $\frac{1}{2}$ | All | All |
| **New Jersey** | $50,000 + $\frac{1}{2}$ | $\frac{1}{3}$ | $50,000 + $\frac{1}{2}$ | All | All |
| **New York** | | | $25,000 + $\frac{1}{2}$ | All | All |
| 1 child | $4,000 + $\frac{1}{2}$ | $4,000 + $\frac{1}{2}$ | | | |
| 2 or more | $4,000 + $\frac{1}{3}$ | $4,000 + $\frac{1}{3}$ | | | |
| **North Carolina** | | | $25,000 + $\frac{1}{2}$ | All | All |
| 1 child | $15,000 + $\frac{1}{2}$ | $15,000 + $\frac{1}{2}$ | | | |
| 2 or more | $15,000 + $\frac{1}{3}$ | $15,000 + $\frac{1}{3}$ | | | |
| **North Dakota** | $50,000 + $\frac{1}{2}$ | $\frac{1}{2}$ | $50,000 + $\frac{1}{2}$ | All | All |
| **Ohio** | | | All | All | All |
| 1 child | $30,000 + $\frac{1}{2}$ | $10,000 + $\frac{1}{2}$ | | | |
| 2 or more | $10,000 + $\frac{1}{3}$ | $10,000 + $\frac{1}{3}$ | | | |
| **Oklahoma** | | | All | All | All |
| Marriage property | $\frac{1}{2}$ | $\frac{1}{2}$ | | | |
| Balance | $\frac{1}{2}$ | Equal shares with children | | | |
| **Oregon** | $\frac{1}{2}$ | $\frac{1}{2}$ | All | All | All |
| **Pennsylvania** | $30,000 + $\frac{1}{2}$ | $\frac{1}{2}$ | $30,000 + $\frac{1}{2}$ | All | All |
| **South Carolina** | | | $\frac{1}{2}$ | $\frac{1}{2}$ | All* |
| 1 child | $\frac{1}{2}$ | $\frac{1}{2}$ | | | |
| 2 or more | $\frac{1}{3}$ | $\frac{1}{3}$ | | | |
| **South Dakota** | | | $100,000 + $\frac{1}{2}$ | $100,000 + $\frac{1}{2}$ | All |
| 1 child | $\frac{1}{2}$ | $\frac{1}{2}$ | | | |
| 2 or more | $\frac{1}{3}$ | $\frac{1}{3}$ | | | |
| **Tennessee** | Homestead + 1 year living allowance ($\frac{1}{3}$ minimum) | | All | All | All |
| **Utah** | $50,000 + $\frac{1}{2}$ | $\frac{1}{2}$ | $100,000 + $\frac{1}{2}$ | All | All |

*If no living grandparents and no living descendants of deceased spouse's grandparents; otherwise, same as previous category.

## *Surviving Spouse Share in All Other States* (continued)

| State | If Deceased Had Children | | If Deceased Had No Children, and There Are | | |
| | Children of Marriage Only | Other Children of Deceased | Living Parents of Deceased | No Living Parents but Living Siblings of Deceased | No Living Parents or Siblings of Deceased |
|---|---|---|---|---|---|
| | | | Then the Surviving Spouse Receives | | |
| **Vermont** | | | $25,000 + $\frac{1}{2}$ | $25,000 + $\frac{1}{2}$ | All* |
| Real property | | | | | |
| 1 child | $\frac{1}{2}$ | $\frac{1}{2}$ | | | |
| 2 or more | $\frac{1}{3}$ | $\frac{1}{3}$ | | | |
| Personal property | $\frac{1}{3}$ | $\frac{1}{3}$ | | | |
| **Virginia** | All | $\frac{1}{3}$ | All | All | All |
| **Wyoming** | $\frac{1}{2}$ | $\frac{1}{2}$ | All | All | All |

*If no living grandparents and no living descendants of deceased spouse's grandparents; otherwise, same as previous category.

# Glossary

**Abatement.** Proportional reduction of general bequests when assets of estate are insufficient to meet such gifts fully.

**Ademption.** Situation occurring when an item of personal property given in a bequest is no longer a part of the final estate, rendering that bequest void.

**Administrator.** A person or corporation appointed by the court to manage the probate of the estate of a person who has died without a valid will.

**Annual exclusion.** The amount that can be given by one person to another in a calendar year without incurring federal gift tax liability. Currently $10,000 per year.

**Appraisal.** A determination of the fair market value of property.

**Attorney-in-fact.** The role of a person you empower to act on your behalf through a power of attorney. This person does not have to be a lawyer.

**Beneficiary.** A person, organization, or institution named in a will to receive a portion of the estate. Also, someone who receives payment from an insurance policy or income from a trust.

**Bequest.** A gift of property made by a valid will.

**Capacity.** A legal adult who is of sound mind and not acting under menace, duress, or undue influence of others has the capacity (ability) to execute a valid will and other legal documents.

**Codicil.** An amendment to an original will that adds to, deletes from, or otherwise changes the provisions of the will; executed and witnessed in the same manner as the original will.

**Common-law marriage.** The cohabitation of a man and a woman appearing to be a legal marriage. In some states, this circumstance may have support and estate distribution implications.

**Community property.** A state-determined method of handling property acquired during marriage. Each spouse has a one-half interest in the subject property, regardless of the spousal financial contribution.

**Contest.** A challenge to the validity of a will, based either on procedural grounds or on questions as to the Testator's capacity.

**Contingent beneficiary.** A person who is designated to become a beneficiary if certain conditions set out in the will are fulfilled.

**Curtesy.** Widower's right to a share of his deceased wife's estate.

**Dependent.** A person who, by virtue of age or physical or mental condition, must rely on another for care and support.

**Devise.** A gift of real estate made by a will.

**Domicile.** Your permanent home, your legal residence; usually where you pay your taxes, vote, and receive correspondence.

**Dower.** Widow's right to a share of her deceased husband's estate.

**Durable power of attorney.** A power of attorney that designates an attorney-in-fact and that is still valid should you become incapacitated or incompetent.

**Escheat.** The taking of estate property by the state when there are no surviving beneficiaries or heirs to receive it.

**Elective share.** The right of a surviving spouse to choose to receive dower or curtesy rights; a share (usually one-half) of the new probate estate rather than the amount in the will.

**Estate.** All assets, real and personal, and all liabilities left by a person who dies.

**Estate tax.** State and federal tax imposed on the transfer of property at death.

**Execute.** To complete and make valid a document by signing it.

**Executor.** A person named by the Testator in a will to administer the estate.

**Fiduciary.** A person who manages property and acts on behalf of another. Executors, Administrators, and trustees are fiduciaries.

**Guardian.** A person who has legal care and control over a minor child or an incompetent adult.

**Heir.** A person who may inherit property through an intestate succession.

**Holographic will.** A will written entirely by hand by the Testator.

**Inheritance tax.** A tax imposed by some states on the receipt of property from an estate. This tax is usually paid by, or on behalf of, the beneficiaries.

**Intestate.** Without a valid will.

**Irrevocable.** Cannot be changed, amended, revoked, or canceled.

**Issue.** Offspring or descendants, such as children and grandchildren.

**Joint property.** All property owned jointly with another party or parties.

**Legacy.** A gift of personal property made by a will.

**Liabilities.** All of a person's mortgages, debts, and obligations.

**Life insurance trust.** A trust funded by the proceeds from life insurance.

**Liquid assets.** Cash, and assets that can be readily converted into cash.

**Living trust.** A trust established during the trustee's life; also known as an *inter vivos* trust.

**Living will.** A signed, witnessed statement requesting that one's life not be prolonged by artificial means in cases of terminal illness or "permanent" unconsciousness.

**Notary.** A person authorized by state commission to certify, or attest to, documents, signatures, and so forth.

**Per capita.** Literally, "by heads"; division in equal shares to surviving named beneficiaries.

**Personal property.** All property owned by a person except real property. Personal property can include personal effects, bank accounts, automobiles, boats, planes, stock, bonds, heirlooms, copyrights, patents, and so on.

**Personal representative.** A state resident who receives legal notices on behalf of another, nonresident person.

**Per stirpes.** Literally, "by the root"; division of property in equal shares to the living descendants of a beneficiary who does not survive the Testator.

**Power of attorney.** A written authorization designating another person to act on your behalf (as your attorney-in-fact).

**Prenuptial agreement.** An agreement executed prior to marriage clarifying individual ownership of assets.

**Probate.** The process of proving the validity of a will in the appropriate court.

**Real property.** All real estate (land, improvements, and buildings) including residences, burial plots, commercial property, condominiums, and time-share units.

**Residue.** The remainder of an estate left after specific bequests have been made.

**Revocable.** Capable of being revoked, canceled, or changed.

**Revoke.** To cancel or terminate.

**Right of survivorship.** The right of a joint property owner to receive full ownership of jointly held property upon the death of the other joint owner. This right is generally set out in the deed or account agreement, and the property does not pass through the probate process.

**Self-proving certificate.** A notarized document stating that a will is properly witnessed.

**Separate property.** Anything that is not community property; often includes property owned before marriage and inheritances received.

**Surety bond.** A bond agreement that pledges to cover losses incurred as a result of willful, illegal administration.

**Testament.** A will, particularly one that deals with the disposition of personal property.

**Testamentary trust.** A trust established by a will.

**Testator.** A person who makes a valid will.

**Title.** Evidence of ownership.

**Trust.** An arrangement whereby a person transfers titled property (assets) to a trustee to hold and manage for the benefit of another person (the trust beneficiary).

**Trustee.** The person or organization that holds title and manages and distributes the trust property in accord with an existing trust agreement.

**Will.** A legal declaration of a person's wishes regarding the disposition of his or her estate after death, usually written and signed by the Testator and attested by witnesses.

**Witness.** A person who sees the maker actually sign a document and so certifies by signature on the document.

# Index

# Record Set

## Using the Forms

### ESTATE INVENTORY SHEETS

This section contains a set of Estate Inventory sheets to assist you in organizing, preparing, and developing your estate plan. Listing the real and personal property of your estate can help you ensure that no assets are overlooked. The categories of property on the estate inventory sheets are transferable to U.S. Estate Tax Return (IRS 706) schedules as indicated in the following table.

### Estate Inventory Sheets

| Category | Transferable to IRS 706 Schedule | Page |
| --- | --- | --- |
| Cash/Notes | C | R-3 |
| Stocks/Bonds | B | R-4 |
| Life insurance | D | R-5 |
| Personal property | F | R-6 |
| Annuities/Pensions | I | R-8 |
| Real property | A | R-9 |
| Joint real property | E | R-10 |
| Farm/Business | A-1 | R-11 |
| Debts (2) | K | R-12 |
| Estate summary (2) | — | R-14 |
| Charitable gifts | O | R-16 |

A two-column format for listing asset values is used on the estate inventory sheets. The two columns can be used to list each spouse's property separately for estate planning purposes. An Executor can also use these estate inventory sheets with one column for date-of-death valuation and the other for alternate valuation (six months after date of death). If you are using the estate inventory sheets for estate planning, pencil entries are recommended, so that future updates can be made easily.

Generally, the assets listed on the first three inventory sheets will be the most liquid and, hence, the source of needed living expenses. When listing the value of personal property, recognize that original cost, replacement cost, market value, and auction value will differ. For property insurance purposes, replacement cost is usual. When valuing estate components, market value or auction value is more realistic. Values listed on the Farm/Business inventory sheet should be based on *use value*, if special valuation is anticipated; otherwise, use market value. Estate summary sheets are included so that the federal estate and state credit estate taxable estates can be calculated for planning purposes or settlement guidance.

## EXECUTOR DATA SHEETS

Following the Estate Inventory sheets, there are two sets of Executor Data sheets. These Executor Data sheets provide space to list the key information your Executor will need. Information regarding organ donation; funeral arrangements; people to contact immediately; biographical background for obituary notices; location of keys, documents, and accounts; and beneficiaries and dependent/guardian concerns should be listed. These Executor Data sheets are perforated so that you can detach them to give to your Executor for use when needed.

# ESTATE INVENTORY

### Bank Accounts

| Checking | Joint acct.? | Account # | Amount | Amount |
|---|---|---|---|---|
| _____ | _____ | _____ | $_____ | $_____ |
| _____ | _____ | _____ | $_____ | $_____ |
| _____ | _____ | _____ | $_____ | $_____ |

### Savings

| | Joint acct.? | Account # | Amount | Amount |
|---|---|---|---|---|
| _____ | _____ | _____ | $_____ | $_____ |
| _____ | _____ | _____ | $_____ | $_____ |
| _____ | _____ | _____ | $_____ | $_____ |

### Certificates

| | | | | |
|---|---|---|---|---|
| _____ | _____ | _____ | $_____ | $_____ |
| _____ | _____ | _____ | $_____ | $_____ |
| _____ | _____ | _____ | $_____ | $_____ |

### IRAs

| | | | | |
|---|---|---|---|---|
| _____ | _____ | _____ | $_____ | $_____ |
| _____ | _____ | _____ | $_____ | $_____ |

### Cash

| | | | | |
|---|---|---|---|---|
| _____ | _____ | _____ | $_____ | $_____ |

### Safe Deposit Box

Location

| | | | | |
|---|---|---|---|---|
| _____ | _____ | _____ | $_____ | $_____ |
| _____ | _____ | _____ | $_____ | $_____ |

### Notes Receivable

Maker_____     $_____     $_____

Address_____

Balance $_____     Security_____

Maker_____     $_____     $_____

Address_____

Balance $_____     Security_____

**Total Cash/Notes**     $_____     $_____

*R-3*

# E S T A T E   I N V E N T O R Y

————————————————— **STOCKS/BONDS** —————————————————

## *Stocks/Mutual Funds*

| Company | Number of shares | CUSIP number | Dollar value | Dollar value |
|---|---|---|---|---|
| _____ | _____ | _____ | $_____ | $_____ |
| _____ | _____ | _____ | $_____ | $_____ |
| _____ | _____ | _____ | $_____ | $_____ |
| _____ | _____ | _____ | $_____ | $_____ |
| _____ | _____ | _____ | $_____ | $_____ |
| _____ | _____ | _____ | $_____ | $_____ |
| _____ | _____ | _____ | $_____ | $_____ |
| _____ | _____ | _____ | $_____ | $_____ |
| _____ | _____ | _____ | $_____ | $_____ |
| _____ | _____ | _____ | $_____ | $_____ |
| _____ | _____ | _____ | $_____ | $_____ |
| _____ | _____ | _____ | $_____ | $_____ |
| _____ | _____ | _____ | $_____ | $_____ |
| _____ | _____ | _____ | $_____ | $_____ |

## *Bonds*

| Company/Government | Cost | Date | Dollar value | Dollar value |
|---|---|---|---|---|
| _____ | $_____ | _____ | $_____ | $_____ |
| _____ | $_____ | _____ | $_____ | $_____ |
| _____ | $_____ | _____ | $_____ | $_____ |
| _____ | $_____ | _____ | $_____ | $_____ |
| _____ | $_____ | _____ | $_____ | $_____ |
| _____ | $_____ | _____ | $_____ | $_____ |
| _____ | $_____ | _____ | $_____ | $_____ |
| _____ | $_____ | _____ | $_____ | $_____ |
| _____ | $_____ | _____ | $_____ | $_____ |
| _____ | $_____ | _____ | $_____ | $_____ |
| _____ | $_____ | _____ | $_____ | $_____ |

**Total Stocks/Bonds**                                        $_____        $_____

# ESTATE INVENTORY

──────────────── **LIFE INSURANCE** ────────────────

**Company**_____ Policy #_____ Amount $_____
Agent/Address_____ Phone_____
Name of
insured_____ Beneficiary_____
Alternate beneficiary_____

**Company**_____ Policy #_____ Amount $_____
Agent/Address_____ Phone_____
Name of
insured_____ Beneficiary_____
Alternate beneficiary_____

**Company**_____ Policy #_____ Amount $_____
Agent/Address_____ Phone_____
Name of
insured_____ Beneficiary_____
Alternate beneficiary_____

**Company**_____ Policy #_____ Amount $_____
Agent/Address_____ Phone_____
Name of
insured_____ Beneficiary_____
Alternate beneficiary_____

**Company**_____ Policy #_____ Amount $_____
Agent/Address_____ Phone_____
Name of
insured_____ Beneficiary_____
Alternate beneficiary_____

**Company**_____ Policy #_____ Amount $_____
Agent/Address_____ Phone_____
Name of
insured_____ Beneficiary_____
Alternate beneficiary_____

**Total Life Insurance**                    $_____        $_____

**————————————— PERSONAL PROPERTY —————————————**

### *Autos, Boats, R.V.s, etc.*

Type_____

Model/ID_____           Value                 Value

Serial #_____       $_____        $_____

Description_____

_____

Type_____

Model/ID_____           Value                 Value

Serial #_____       $_____        $_____

Description_____

_____

Type_____

Model/ID_____           Value                 Value

Serial #_____       $_____        $_____

Description_____

_____

Type_____

Model/ID_____           Value                 Value

Serial #_____       $_____        $_____

Description_____

_____

### *Household Effects and Furniture*

Description                    Value                 Value

_____       $_____        $_____

_____       $_____        $_____

_____       $_____        $_____

_____       $_____        $_____

_____       $_____        $_____

_____       $_____        $_____

_____       $_____        $_____

_____       $_____        $_____

(*continued*)

# ESTATE INVENTORY

### *Jewelry*

| Description | Value | Value |
|---|---|---|
| _____ | $_____ | $_____ |
| _____ | $_____ | $_____ |
| _____ | $_____ | $_____ |
| _____ | $_____ | $_____ |
| _____ | $_____ | $_____ |
| _____ | $_____ | $_____ |
| _____ | $_____ | $_____ |

### *Tools/Hobby/Sporting Goods*

| Description | Value | Value |
|---|---|---|
| _____ | $_____ | $_____ |
| _____ | $_____ | $_____ |
| _____ | $_____ | $_____ |

### *Heirlooms and Collections*

| Description | Value | Value |
|---|---|---|
| _____ | $_____ | $_____ |
| _____ | $_____ | $_____ |
| _____ | $_____ | $_____ |

### *Antiques*

| Description | Value | Value |
|---|---|---|
| _____ | $_____ | $_____ |
| _____ | $_____ | $_____ |
| _____ | $_____ | $_____ |

### *Miscellaneous*

| Description | Value | Value |
|---|---|---|
| _____ | $_____ | $_____ |
| _____ | $_____ | $_____ |
| _____ | $_____ | $_____ |

**Total Personal Property**   $_____   $_____

# ESTATE INVENTORY

**————— ANNUITIES/PENSIONS —————**

**Company**_____ #_____

Agent_____ Amount $_____

Owner_____ Beneficiary_____

**Company**_____ #_____

Agent_____ Amount $_____

Owner_____ Beneficiary_____

**Company**_____ #_____

Agent_____ Amount $_____

Owner_____ Beneficiary_____

**Company**_____ #_____

Agent_____ Amount $_____

Owner_____ Beneficiary_____

**Company**_____ #_____

Agent_____ Amount $_____

Owner_____ Beneficiary_____

**Company**_____ #_____

Agent_____ Amount $_____

Owner_____ Beneficiary_____

**Company**_____ #_____

Agent_____ Amount $_____

Owner_____ Beneficiary_____

**Company**_____ #_____

Agent_____ Amount $_____

Owner_____ Beneficiary_____

**Company**_____ #_____

Agent_____ Amount $_____

Owner_____ Beneficiary_____

**Total Annuities/Pensions**        $_____    $_____

# E S T A T E   I N V E N T O R Y

───────────────── **REAL PROPERTY** ─────────────────

### *Residence*

House □   Condominium □   Co-op □   Other □

Description_____

_____

|  |  |  |
|---|---|---|
| Address_____ | Market value | Market value |
| _____ | $_____ | $_____ |

Deed in name of_____

Jointly owned □   Community property □   Co-owned □

Joint owner/Co-owner_____

### *Second/Vacation Home*

Description_____

_____   Property #_____

|  |  |  |
|---|---|---|
| Address_____ | Market value | Market value |
| _____ | $_____ | $_____ |

Deed in name of_____

Jointly owned □   Community property □   Co-owned □

Joint owner/Co-owner_____

### *Commercial/Rental Property*

Description_____

_____   Property #_____

|  |  |  |
|---|---|---|
| Address_____ | Market value | Market value |
| _____ | $_____ | $_____ |

Deed in name of_____

Jointly owned □   Co-owned □   Partnership □   Corporation □   Other □

Joint/Co-owner(s)_____

_____

**Total Real Property**        $_____        $_____

*R-9*

# ESTATE INVENTORY

─────────────── **JOINT REAL PROPERTY** ───────────────

### *Residence*

House ☐   Condominium ☐   Co-op ☐   Other ☐

Description_____

_____

|  | Market value | Market value |
|---|---|---|
| Address_____ | $_____ | $_____ |

_____

Deed in name of_____

Jointly owned ☐   Community property ☐   Co-owned ☐

Joint owner/Co-owner_____

### *Second/Vacation Home*

Description_____

_____  Property #_____

_____

|  | Market value | Market value |
|---|---|---|
| Address_____ | $_____ | $_____ |

_____

Deed in name of_____

Jointly owned ☐   Community property ☐   Co-owned ☐

Joint owner/Co-owner_____

### *Commercial/Rental Property*

Description_____

_____  Property #_____

_____

|  | Market value | Market value |
|---|---|---|
| Address_____ | $_____ | $_____ |

_____

Deed in name of_____

Jointly owned ☐   Co-owned ☐   Partnership ☐   Corporation ☐   Other ☐

Joint/Co-owner(s)_____

_____

**Total Joint Real Property**          $_____          $_____

*R-10*

# ESTATE INVENTORY

## FARM/BUSINESS

### Farm

| | | |
|---|---|---|
| Real estate | $_____ | $_____ |
|   Market value | $_____ | $_____ |
|   Farm use value | $_____ | $_____ |
| Improvements | $_____ | $_____ |
| Equipment | $_____ | $_____ |
| Supplies | $_____ | $_____ |
| Livestock | $_____ | $_____ |
| Crops | $_____ | $_____ |
| **Totals—Market value** | $_____ | $_____ |
| **Totals—Farm use value** | $_____ | $_____ |

Real estate % of Market value      _____%

Real estate % of Farm use value     _____%

Owners_____

_____

Operator(s)_____

### Business

| | | |
|---|---|---|
| Real estate | $_____ | $_____ |
|   Market value | $_____ | $_____ |
|   Business use value | $_____ | $_____ |
| Improvements | $_____ | $_____ |
| Equipment | $_____ | $_____ |
| Supplies | $_____ | $_____ |
| Other | $_____ | $_____ |
| **Totals—Market value** | $_____ | $_____ |
| **Totals—Business use value** | $_____ | $_____ |

Real estate % of Market value      _____%

Real estate % of Business use value    _____%

Owners_____

_____

Management_____

Buy–sell agreement               Yes___   No___

| | | |
|---|---|---|
| Business life insurance policy | $_____ | $_____ |
| | $_____ | $_____ |
| **Total Business Life Insurance** | $_____ | $_____ |

# E S T A T E   I N V E N T O R Y

## DEBTS

### *Mortgages/Notes*

Type_____ Original balance $_____

Security_____

Mortage/Note holder_____

Address_____

Location of document_____

Type_____ Original balance $_____

Security_____

Mortgage/Note holder_____

Address_____

Location of document_____

Type_____ Original balance $_____

Security_____

Mortgage/Note holder_____

Address_____

Location of document_____

### *Other Debts*

| Account | Number | Balance |
|---------|--------|---------|
| _____ | _____ | $_____ |
| _____ | _____ | $_____ |
| _____ | _____ | $_____ |
| _____ | _____ | $_____ |
| _____ | _____ | $_____ |
| _____ | _____ | $_____ |
| _____ | _____ | $_____ |
| _____ | _____ | $_____ |
| _____ | _____ | $_____ |
| _____ | _____ | $_____ |
| _____ | _____ | $_____ |

**Total Debts**                                        $_____

# E S T A T E    I N V E N T O R Y

## ———————————————— DEBTS ————————————————

### Mortgages/Notes

Type_____ Original balance $_____

Security_____

Mortage/Note holder_____

Address_____

Location of document_____

Type_____ Original balance $_____

Security_____

Mortgage/Note holder_____

Address_____

Location of document_____

Type_____ Original balance $_____

Security_____

Mortgage/Note holder_____

Address_____

Location of document_____

### Other Debts

| Account | Number | Balance |
|---|---|---|
| _____ | _____ | $_____ |
| _____ | _____ | $_____ |
| _____ | _____ | $_____ |
| _____ | _____ | $_____ |
| _____ | _____ | $_____ |
| _____ | _____ | $_____ |
| _____ | _____ | $_____ |
| _____ | _____ | $_____ |
| _____ | _____ | $_____ |
| _____ | _____ | $_____ |
| _____ | _____ | $_____ |
| **Total Debts** | | $_____ |

# E S T A T E  I N V E N T O R Y

## ——————— ESTATE SUMMARY ———————

### *Estate Component Totals*

| | | |
|---|---|---|
| Cash/Notes | $_____ | $_____ |
| Stocks/Bonds | $_____ | $_____ |
| Life Insurance | $_____ | $_____ |
| Personal Property | $_____ | $_____ |
| Annuities/Pensions | $_____ | $_____ |
| Real Property | $_____ | $_____ |
| Joint Real Property | $_____ | $_____ |
| Farm/Business | $_____ | $_____ |
| Inheritance | $_____ | $_____ |
| Gross estate totals | $_____ | $_____ |
| (less debts) | $ (_____) | $ (_____) |
| Balance | $_____ | $_____ |
| (less charitable gifts) | $ (_____) | $ (_____) |
| Balance | $_____ | $_____ |
| (less settlement cost estimate) | $ (_____) | $ (_____) |
| Actual estate before taxes | $_____ | $_____ |
| (less federal estate tax deduction) | $ (600,000) | $ (600,000) |
| Federal taxable estate | $_____ | $_____ |

*NOTE:* If there is a federal taxable estate, an IRS 706 Return must be filed. A surviving spouse may use the amount of the marital deduction (Schedule M) to reduce the federal taxable estate to zero. Check with State Department of Taxation regarding other state estate, inheritance, gift and/or generation-skip tax liabilities.

| | | |
|---|---|---|
| Federal taxable estate (less state credit estate tax deduction) | $ ( 60,000) | $ ( 60,000) |
| State credit estate taxable estate | $_____ | $_____ |

R-14

# ESTATE INVENTORY

## ————— ESTATE SUMMARY —————

**Estate Component Totals**

| | | |
|---|---|---|
| Cash/Notes | $_____ | $_____ |
| Stocks/Bonds | $_____ | $_____ |
| Life Insurance | $_____ | $_____ |
| Personal Property | $_____ | $_____ |
| Annuities/Pensions | $_____ | $_____ |
| Real Property | $_____ | $_____ |
| Joint Real Property | $_____ | $_____ |
| Farm/Business | $_____ | $_____ |
| Inheritance _____ | $_____ | $_____ |
| Gross estate totals | $_____ | $_____ |
| (less debts) _____ | $ (_____) | $ (_____) |
| Balance | $_____ | $_____ |
| (less charitable gifts) _____ | $ (_____) | $ (_____) |
| Balance | $_____ | $_____ |
| (less settlement cost estimate) _____ | $ (_____) | $ (_____) |
| Actual estate before taxes | $_____ | $_____ |
| (less federal estate tax deduction) _____ | $_____ (600,000) | $_____ (600,000) |
| Federal taxable estate | $_____ | $_____ |

*NOTE:* If there is a federal taxable estate, an IRS 706 Return must be filed. A surviving spouse may use the amount of the marital deduction (Schedule M) to reduce the federal taxable estate to zero. Check with State Department of Taxation regarding other state estate, inheritance, gift and/or generation-skip tax liabilities.

| | | |
|---|---|---|
| Federal taxable estate (less state credit estate tax deduction) _____ | $_____ ( 60,000) | $_____ ( 60,000) |
| State credit estate taxable estate | $_____ | $_____ |

—————————————————— **CHARITABLE GIFTS** ——————————————————

### *Church*

Full name                               Address                        Bequest(s)

_____   _____   _____

_____   _____   _____

_____   _____   _____

_____   _____   _____

### *Schools, Colleges*

Full name                               Address                        Bequest(s)

_____   _____   _____

_____   _____   _____

_____   _____   _____

_____   _____   _____

### *Charities, Institutions*

Full name                               Address                        Bequest(s)

_____   _____   _____

_____   _____   _____

_____   _____   _____

_____   _____   _____

_____   _____   _____

### *Other Nonprofit Organizations*

Full name                               Address                        Bequest(s)

_____   _____   _____

_____   _____   _____

_____   _____   _____

**Total Charitable Gifts**                      $_____     $_____

# *Executor Data*

Following are two detachable sets of Executor Data sheets. These sheets will enable you to organize and record information that will be of vital importance to your Executor. Each set has one sheet for each of these categories:

Immediate.

Contacts.

Personal.

Final arrangements.

Beneficiaries.

Dependents/Guardians.

# E X E C U T O R   D A T A

**———————————— IMMEDIATE ————————————**

## Location of Documents/Keys

Location of will_____

Date executed_____ # of Pages _____

Other documents_____

_____

_____

_____

Keys/Safety deposit box_____

_____

_____

_____

## Burial/Funeral

Responsible person/Organization

Name_____

Address_____

Phone_____

Interment ☐   Cremation ☐   Crypt ☐   Other ☐

Service Type: Religious ☐   Fraternal ☐   Other ☐

Cemetery/Columbarium_____

_____

## Body/Eye/Organ Donations

Organization/Group_____

Contact_____

Phone_____

Address_____

Donation_____

Organization/Group_____

Contact_____

Address_____

Phone_____

Donation_____

# E X E C U T O R  D A T A

## —————— CONTACTS ——————

**Accountant**———————————————————— Phone————————————

Address————————————————————————————————

**Attorney**———————————————————— Phone————————————

Address————————————————————————————————

**Banker**———————————————————— Phone————————————

Address————————————————————————————————

**Clergyman**———————————————————— Phone————————————

Address————————————————————————————————

**Doctor**———————————————————— Phone————————————

Address————————————————————————————————

**Executor**———————————————————— Phone————————————

Address————————————————————————————————

**Alternate Executor**———————————————————— Phone————————————

Address————————————————————————————————

**Insurance agent**———————————————————— Phone————————————

Address————————————————————————————————

**Insurance agent**———————————————————— Phone————————————

Address————————————————————————————————

**Trustee**———————————————————— Phone————————————

Address————————————————————————————————


### *Relatives/Friends*

**Name**———————————————————— Phone————————————

Address————————————————————————————————

**Name**———————————————————— Phone————————————

Address————————————————————————————————

**Name**———————————————————— Phone————————————

Address————————————————————————————————

**Name**———————————————————— Phone————————————

Address————————————————————————————————

─────────────────── **PERSONAL** ───────────────────

Full name_____ Birth date_____

Address_____

_____

Birthplace_____

Social security #_____ Medicare #_____

Military service #_____ Discharge date_____

Father's name_____ Birth date_____

Date deceased_____ Birthplace_____

Mother's maiden name_____ Birth date_____

Date deceased_____ Birthplace_____

Married □   Divorced □   Separated □   Widowed □   Single □   Remarried □

Spouse (name)_____ Marriage date_____

Social security #_____ Medicare #_____

Membership (Religious/Fraternal/Social, Other)_____

_____

_____

*Children*

Name_____ Birth date_____

Address_____

Name_____ Birth date_____

Address_____

Name_____ Birth date_____

Address_____

Name_____ Birth date_____

Address_____

Name_____ Birth date_____

Address_____

———————————————— **FINAL ARRANGEMENTS** ————————————————

Person responsible_____ Phone_____

Address_____

Alternate person_____ Phone_____

Funeral home (name)_____ Phone_____

Address_____

Location of service_____ Viewing: Yes ☐   No ☐

Address_____

Service type: Religious ☐   Military ☐   Fraternal ☐   Memorial ☐

Person officiating_____ Phone_____

Cemetery_____

Location_____

Section_____ Plot #_____

Interment_____ Entombment_____ Cremation_____

Location of deed_____

Music/Reading selections_____

_____

_____

_____

Flowers/Memorials_____

_____

Pallbearers                                        (Honorary)

_____        _____

_____        _____

_____        _____

_____        _____

_____        _____

*R-22*

# E X E C U T O R  D A T A

## BENEFICIARIES

**Name**_____ Relationship_____

**Address**_____ Phone_____

**Bequest(s)**_____
_____

**Name**_____ Relationship_____

**Address**_____ Phone_____

**Bequest(s)**_____
_____

**Name**_____ Relationship_____

**Address**_____ Phone_____

**Bequest(s)**_____
_____

**Name**_____ Relationship_____

**Address**_____ Phone_____

**Bequest(s)**_____
_____

**Name**_____ Relationship_____

**Address**_____ Phone_____

**Bequest(s)**_____
_____

**Name**_____ Relationship_____

**Address**_____ Phone_____

**Bequest(s)**_____
_____

**Name**_____ Relationship_____

**Address**_____ Phone_____

**Bequest(s)**_____
_____

**Name**_____ Relationship_____

**Address**_____ Phone_____

**Bequest(s)**_____
_____

# EXECUTOR DATA

## DEPENDENTS/GUARDIANS

### Guardian(s)

Name_____ Relationship_____

Address_____

Name_____ Relationship_____

Address_____

### Dependent Name

| | Birth date | S.S. # |
|---|---|---|
| 1. _____ | _____ | _____ |
| 2. _____ | _____ | _____ |
| 3. _____ | _____ | _____ |
| 4. _____ | _____ | _____ |

### Medical Information

| | Blood type | Doctor |
|---|---|---|
| 1. _____ | _____ | _____ |
| 2. _____ | _____ | _____ |
| 3. _____ | _____ | _____ |
| 4. _____ | _____ | _____ |

Health Insurance (Company/Policy #) _____

### Special Instructions (Education, Religion, Guardianship agreement)

_____
_____
_____
_____

### Assets (Accounts, Stocks, Bonds, Other) Manager: Guardian ☐ Executor ☐ Trustee ☐ Bank ☐ Other ☐

_____
_____
_____

### Insurance

Company/Agent_____ Amt./Type_____

Policy #_____ Address/Phone_____

Company/Agent_____ Amt./Type_____

Policy #_____ Address/Phone_____

# E X E C U T O R    D A T A

────────────── **IMMEDIATE** ──────────────

## *Location of Documents/Keys*

Location of will_____

Date executed_____ # of Pages _____

Other documents_____

_____

_____

_____

Keys/Safety deposit box_____

_____

_____

_____

## *Burial/Funeral*

Responsible person/Organization

Name_____

Address_____

Phone_____

Interment ☐   Cremation ☐   Crypt ☐   Other ☐

Service Type: Religious ☐   Fraternal ☐   Other ☐

Cemetery/Columbarium_____

_____

## *Body/Eye/Organ Donations*

Organization/Group_____

Contact_____

Phone_____

Address_____

Donation_____

Organization/Group_____

Contact_____

Address_____

Phone_____

Donation_____

# EXECUTOR DATA

## CONTACTS

**Accountant**_____ Phone_____
Address_____

**Attorney**_____ Phone_____
Address_____

**Banker**_____ Phone_____
Address_____

**Clergyman**_____ Phone_____
Address_____

**Doctor**_____ Phone_____
Address_____

**Executor**_____ Phone_____
Address_____

**Alternate Executor**_____ Phone_____
Address_____

**Insurance agent**_____ Phone_____
Address_____

**Insurance agent**_____ Phone_____
Address_____

**Trustee**_____ Phone_____
Address_____


### Relatives/Friends

**Name**_____ Phone_____
Address_____

**Name**_____ Phone_____
Address_____

**Name**_____ Phone_____
Address_____

**Name**_____ Phone_____
Address_____

# E X E C U T O R   D A T A

———————————————— **PERSONAL** ————————————————

Full name_____ Birth date_____

Address_____

_____

Birthplace_____

Social security #_____ Medicare #_____

Military service #_____ Discharge date_____

Father's name_____ Birth date_____

Date deceased_____ Birthplace_____

Mother's maiden name_____ Birth date_____

Date deceased_____ Birthplace_____

Married ☐   Divorced ☐   Separated ☐   Widowed ☐   Single ☐   Remarried ☐

Spouse (name)_____ Marriage date_____

Social security #_____ Medicare #_____

Membership (Religious/Fraternal/Social, Other)_____

_____

_____

*Children*

Name_____ Birth date_____

Address_____

Name_____ Birth date_____

Address_____

Name_____ Birth date_____

Address_____

Name_____ Birth date_____

Address_____

Name_____ Birth date_____

Address_____

───────────────── **FINAL ARRANGEMENTS** ─────────────────

Person responsible_____ Phone_____

Address_____

Alternate person_____ Phone_____

Funeral home (name)_____ Phone_____

Address_____

Location of service_____ Viewing: Yes ☐   No ☐

Address_____

Service type: Religious ☐   Military ☐   Fraternal ☐   Memorial ☐

Person officiating_____ Phone_____

Cemetery_____

Location_____

Section_____ Plot #_____

Interment_____ Entombment_____ Cremation_____

Location of deed_____

Music/Reading selections_____

_____

_____

_____

Flowers/Memorials_____

_____

Pallbearers                              (Honorary)

_____          _____

_____          _____

_____          _____

_____          _____

_____          _____

# E X E C U T O R  D A T A

## BENEFICIARIES

**Name**_____ Relationship_____

**Address**_____ Phone_____

**Bequest(s)**_____

_____

**Name**_____ Relationship_____

**Address**_____ Phone_____

**Bequest(s)**_____

_____

**Name**_____ Relationship_____

**Address**_____ Phone_____

**Bequest(s)**_____

_____

**Name**_____ Relationship_____

**Address**_____ Phone_____

**Bequest(s)**_____

_____

**Name**_____ Relationship_____

**Address**_____ Phone_____

**Bequest(s)**_____

_____

**Name**_____ Relationship_____

**Address**_____ Phone_____

**Bequest(s)**_____

_____

**Name**_____ Relationship_____

**Address**_____ Phone_____

**Bequest(s)**_____

_____

**Name**_____ Relationship_____

**Address**_____ Phone_____

**Bequest(s)**_____

_____

# EXECUTOR DATA

## —— DEPENDENTS/GUARDIANS ——

### Guardian(s)

Name_____ Relationship_____

Address_____

Name_____ Relationship_____

Address_____

### Dependent Name

|  | Birth date | S.S. # |
|---|---|---|
| 1. _____ | _____ | _____ |
| 2. _____ | _____ | _____ |
| 3. _____ | _____ | _____ |
| 4. _____ | _____ | _____ |

### Medical Information

|  | Blood type | Doctor |
|---|---|---|
| 1. _____ | _____ | _____ |
| 2. _____ | _____ | _____ |
| 3. _____ | _____ | _____ |
| 4. _____ | _____ | _____ |

Health Insurance (Company/Policy #) _____

### Special Instructions (Education, Religion, Guardianship agreement)

_____

_____

_____

_____

### Assets (Accounts, Stocks, Bonds, Other) Manager: Guardian ☐  Executor ☐  Trustee ☐  Bank ☐  Other ☐

_____

_____

_____

### Insurance

Company/Agent_____ Amt./Type_____

Policy #_____ Address/Phone_____

Company/Agent_____ Amt./Type_____

Policy #_____ Address/Phone_____

# Document Set

## Using the Detachable Forms

There are a total of eight will forms in this section. They are perforated for easy removal and use. The completed forms, filled in in ink or on a typewriter, may be used as original documents. The forms may also be used as a guide if you prefer to type your own or need additional documents. Duplicate forms are provided so that you may revise or amend your estate plan when needed. Forms should be completed carefully with no crossed out words or erasures. All signatures should be written in ink. If you desire copies of your will and other documents, make them *before* you sign the originals. Never sign anything but the original document(s). *Do not* sign copies. Preparing a draft outline of your will can help avoid mistakes when you prepare the final document.

Be sure that your Executor, alternate Executor, guardian, and/or other persons involved with your estate plan are fully informed and consent to act on your behalf on mutually agreed-on terms. It is recommended that your chosen agents be given specific information as listed in the Executor Data sheets in the preceding Record Set. Detailed information allows your Executor to act effectively and efficiently in settling your estate.

### Forms Provided

Last will and testament (one-page form)—four copies.

Last will and testament (two-page form)—two copies.

Last will and testament (three-page form)—two copies.

Will self-proving certificate—four copies.

Codicil—two copies.

Codicil self-proving certificate—two copies.

Letter of instructions—two copies.

## LAST WILL AND TESTAMENT

The three sets of will forms offer space to set out your plans, from a single bequest to extensive gifts or instructions. The first two sets of (one- and two-page) forms contain printed provisions that save expense to the estate. The following provisions are usually appropriate for all estates that name a beneficiary or other trusted person as Executor.

- The EXECUTOR named shall not be required to post surety bond.
- I direct that no outside appraisal be made of my estate unless required for estate tax purposes.

The last set of forms does not contain these provisions, although they may be written or typed on the forms, if desired. This last set has unnumbered pages, which may be used in sets or combined as needed. Be sure to indicate the page number and page total at the bottom of each page. You and your witnesses should also initial each page in the space provided at the bottom when you execute your will. All multiple-page wills should be fastened together before execution. Remember, you can't add pages after you've executed your will.

If you live in or have property in the states of Louisiana or Vermont, you must have three witnesses; everywhere else two witnesses are sufficient. Sign and date documents in front of all witnesses together at the same time and have them sign, date, and list their addresses on the document. You may keep the specific contents of wills and codicils confidential—your witnesses are attesting to your intent to make a will, not to the content of it. Remember, witnesses should *not* be relatives or others with an interest in your estate. Proper witness procedure should always be followed when executing your will or other documents.

## WILL SELF-PROVING CERTIFICATE

Self-proving is an optional step that does not affect the validity of your will. A self-proving certificate, properly completed and notarized, eliminates the need for witnesses to be contacted when the will is presented for probate. The four self-proving certificates included may be completed by a notary public and attached to your will. To self-prove your will, you must appear before the notary with your witnesses and your original will. The notary can complete the self-proving certificate; after all have signed, the notary notarizes and seals the document before attaching it to your will. Be sure the expiration date of the notary commission is listed and that the notary seal is affixed. All states except Illinois, Vermont, and West Virginia recognize properly notarized self-proving certificates.

## *CODICIL*

Two codicil forms are included for use if minor amendments to your will are needed. Have your original will before you when you prepare your codicil to verify its date of execution. Witness procedure for a codicil is the same as for a will.

## *CODICIL SELF-PROVING CERTIFICATE*

A codicil may be self-proved in the same manner as a will in those states that recognize self-proving certificates. A self-proved codicil self-proves the will it amends. Note that the date of the original will must be filled in on the codicil self-proving certificate.

## *LETTER OF INSTRUCTIONS*

Letters of instructions are provided to convey additional information to your Executor, or appointed guardian, if required. You should date the letter of instructions and, if it contains specific directions regarding your estate, refer to the document by its date in your will. Remember, your will must set out the actual gifts of property or assets. Letters of instructions may contain messages or descriptions of heirlooms or property that are too lengthy or personal to be included in your will.

# LAST WILL AND TESTAMENT

I, _____ , resident

of the _____ of _____ in the State of _____ ,

being of sound mind, do make and declare the following to be my LAST WILL AND TESTAMENT and expressly revoke all my prior wills and codicils and certify that I am not acting under undue influence, duress or menace.

## I. EXECUTOR

I appoint _____ EXECUTOR
of this my LAST WILL AND TESTAMENT. If this EXECUTOR is unable to serve for any reason,

then I appoint _____ EXECUTOR.
The EXECUTOR is empowered to carry out all provisions of this WILL.
The EXECUTOR shall have all statutory powers available under State law.
The EXECUTOR named shall not be required to post surety bond. I direct that no outside appraisal be made of my estate, unless required for estate tax purposes.

## II. BEQUESTS

IN WITNESS WHEREOF, I have hereunto set my hand this_____ day
of _____ , 19 _____ .

_____
*(Testator signature)*

# III. WITNESSED

This LAST WILL AND TESTAMENT of _____
was signed and declared to be his/her LAST WILL AND TESTAMENT in our presence at his/her request
and in his/her presence and the presence of each other as witnesses this _____

day of _____ , 19 _____ .

_____     _____
*(Witness signature)*                                              *(Address)*

_____     _____
*(Witness signature)*                                              *(Address)*

_____     _____
*(Witness signature)*                                              *(Address)*

# LAST WILL AND TESTAMENT

I, _____ , resident

of the _____ of _____ in the State of _____ ,

being of sound mind, do make and declare the following to be my LAST WILL AND TESTAMENT and expressly revoke all my prior wills and codicils and certify that I am not acting under undue influence, duress or menace.

## I. EXECUTOR

I appoint _____ EXECUTOR
of this my LAST WILL AND TESTAMENT. If this EXECUTOR is unable to serve for any reason,

then I appoint _____ EXECUTOR.

The EXECUTOR is empowered to carry out all provisions of this WILL.

The EXECUTOR shall have all statutory powers available under State law.

The EXECUTOR named shall not be required to post surety bond. I direct that no outside appraisal be made of my estate, unless required for estate tax purposes.

## II. BEQUESTS

IN WITNESS WHEREOF, I have hereunto set my hand this_____ day

of _____ , 19 _____ .

_____
*(Testator signature)*

# III. WITNESSED

This LAST WILL AND TESTAMENT of _____
was signed and declared to be his/her LAST WILL AND TESTAMENT in our presence at his/her request
and in his/her presence and the presence of each other as witnesses this _____

day of _____ , 19 _____ .

_____          _____
*(Witness signature)*                          *(Address)*

_____          _____
*(Witness signature)*                          *(Address)*

_____          _____
*(Witness signature)*                          *(Address)*

# LAST WILL AND TESTAMENT

I, _____ , resident

of the _____ of _____ in the State of _____ ,

being of sound mind, do make and declare the following to be my LAST WILL AND TESTAMENT
and expressly revoke all my prior wills and codicils and certify that I am not acting under undue
influence, duress or menace.

## I. EXECUTOR

I appoint _____ EXECUTOR
of this my LAST WILL AND TESTAMENT. If this EXECUTOR is unable to serve for any reason,

then I appoint _____ EXECUTOR.

The EXECUTOR is empowered to carry out all provisions of this WILL.

The EXECUTOR shall have all statutory powers available under State law.

The EXECUTOR named shall not be required to post surety bond. I direct that no outside appraisal
be made of my estate, unless required for estate tax purposes.

## II. BEQUESTS

IN WITNESS WHEREOF, I have hereunto set my hand this_____ day

of _____ , 19 _____ .

_____
*(Testator signature)*

# III. WITNESSED

This LAST WILL AND TESTAMENT of _____.
was signed and declared to be his/her LAST WILL AND TESTAMENT in our presence at his/her request
and in his/her presence and the presence of each other as witnesses this _____

day of _____ , 19 _____ .

_____     _____
*(Witness signature)*                                    *(Address)*

_____     _____
*(Witness signature)*                                    *(Address)*

_____     _____
*(Witness signature)*                                    *(Address)*

# LAST WILL AND TESTAMENT

I, _____ , resident

of the _____ of _____ in the State of _____ ,

being of sound mind, do make and declare the following to be my LAST WILL AND TESTAMENT
and expressly revoke all my prior wills and codicils and certify that I am not acting under undue
influence, duress or menace.

## I. EXECUTOR

I appoint _____ EXECUTOR
of this my LAST WILL AND TESTAMENT. If this EXECUTOR is unable to serve for any reason,

then I appoint _____ EXECUTOR.
The EXECUTOR is empowered to carry out all provisions of this WILL.
The EXECUTOR shall have all statutory powers available under State law.
The EXECUTOR named shall not be required to post surety bond. I direct that no outside appraisal
be made of my estate, unless required for estate tax purposes.

## II. BEQUESTS

IN WITNESS WHEREOF, I have hereunto set my hand this_____ day

of _____ , 19 _____ .

_____
*(Testator signature)*

# III. WITNESSED

This LAST WILL AND TESTAMENT of _____
was signed and declared to be his/her LAST WILL AND TESTAMENT in our presence at his/her request
and in his/her presence and the presence of each other as witnesses this _____

day of _____ , 19 _____ .

_____        _____
*(Witness signature)*                                             *(Address)*

_____        _____
*(Witness signature)*                                             *(Address)*

_____        _____
*(Witness signature)*                                             *(Address)*

# LAST WILL AND TESTAMENT

I, _____ , resident

of the _____ of _____ in the State of _____ ,

being of sound mind, do make and declare the following to be my LAST WILL AND TESTAMENT
and expressly revoke all my prior wills and codicils and certify that I am not acting under undue
influence, duress or menace.

## I. EXECUTOR

I appoint _____ EXECUTOR
of this my LAST WILL AND TESTAMENT. If this EXECUTOR is unable to serve for any reason,

then I appoint _____ EXECUTOR.
The EXECUTOR is empowered to carry out all provisions of this WILL.
The EXECUTOR shall have all statutory powers available under State law.
The EXECUTOR named shall not be required to post surety bond. I direct that no outside appraisal
be made of my estate, unless required for estate tax purposes.

## II. BEQUESTS

IN WITNESS WHEREOF, I have hereunto set my hand this_____ day
of  _____ , 19 _____ .

_____
*(Testator signature)*

# III. WITNESSED

This LAST WILL AND TESTAMENT of _____
was signed and declared to be his/her LAST WILL AND TESTAMENT in our presence at his/her request
and in his/her presence and the presence of each other as witnesses this _____

day of _____ , 19 _____ .

_____
*(Witness signature)*                                  *(Address)*

_____
*(Witness signature)*                                  *(Address)*

_____
*(Witness signature)*                                  *(Address)*

# LAST WILL AND TESTAMENT

I, _____ , resident

of the _____ of _____ in the State of _____ ,

being of sound mind, do make and declare the following to be my LAST WILL AND TESTAMENT
and expressly revoke all my prior wills and codicils and certify that I am not acting under undue
influence, duress or menace.

## I. EXECUTOR

I appoint _____ EXECUTOR
of this my LAST WILL AND TESTAMENT. If this EXECUTOR is unable to serve for any reason,

then I appoint _____ EXECUTOR.
The EXECUTOR is empowered to carry out all provisions of this WILL.
The EXECUTOR shall have all statutory powers available under State law.
The EXECUTOR named shall not be required to post surety bond. I direct that no outside appraisal
be made of my estate, unless required for estate tax purposes.

## II. BEQUESTS

IN WITNESS WHEREOF, I have hereunto set my hand this_____ day

of _____ , 19 _____ .

_____
(Testator signature)

# III. WITNESSED

This LAST WILL AND TESTAMENT of _____
was signed and declared to be his/her LAST WILL AND TESTAMENT in our presence at his/her request
and in his/her presence and the presence of each other as witnesses this _____

day of _____ , 19 _____ .

_____
(Witness signature)                                          (Address)

_____
(Witness signature)                                          (Address)

_____
(Witness signature)                                          (Address)

# LAST WILL AND TESTAMENT

I, _____ , resident
of the _____ of _____ in the State of _____ ,
being of sound mind, do make and declare the following to be my LAST WILL AND TESTAMENT
and expressly revoke all my prior wills and codicils and certify that I am not acting under undue
influence, duress or menace.

## I. EXECUTOR

I appoint _____ EXECUTOR
of this, my LAST WILL AND TESTAMENT. If this EXECUTOR is unable to serve for any reason,

then I appoint _____ EXECUTOR.
The EXECUTOR is empowered to carry out all provisions of this WILL.
The EXECUTOR shall have all statutory powers available under State law.

## II. BEQUESTS

INITIALS _____     _____
                (Testator)                                    (Witnesses)
                        Page _____ of _____

INITIALS _____
            *(Testator)*

_____
                *(Witnesses)*

Page _____ of _____

IN WITNESS WHEREOF, I have hereunto set my hand this _____ day

of _____ , 19 _____ .

_____

*(Testator signature)*

# III. WITNESSED

This LAST WILL AND TESTAMENT of _____
was signed and declared to be his/her LAST WILL AND TESTAMENT in our presence at his/her request
and in his/her presence and the presence of each other as witnesses this _____

day of _____ , 19 _____ .

_____ _____
*(Witness signature)*                                      *(Address)*

_____ _____
*(Witness signature)*                                      *(Address)*

_____ _____
*(Witness signature)*                                      *(Address)*

Page _____ of _____

# LAST WILL AND TESTAMENT

I, _____ , resident
of the _____ of _____ in the State of _____ ,
being of sound mind, do make and declare the following to be my LAST WILL AND TESTAMENT
and expressly revoke all my prior wills and codicils and certify that I am not acting under undue
influence, duress or menace.

## I. EXECUTOR

I appoint _____ EXECUTOR
of this, my LAST WILL AND TESTAMENT. If this EXECUTOR is unable to serve for any reason,

then I appoint _____ EXECUTOR.
The EXECUTOR is empowered to carry out all provisions of this WILL.
The EXECUTOR shall have all statutory powers available under State law.

## II. BEQUESTS

INITIALS _____
                 *(Testator)*      _____
                                                                    *(Witnesses)*
                          Page \_\_\_\_\_ of _____

INITIALS _____ _____
                (Testator)                                                    (Witnesses)
                          Page _____ of _____

IN WITNESS WHEREOF, I have hereunto set my hand this_____ day

of _____ , 19 _____ .

_____
(Testator signature)

# III. WITNESSED

This LAST WILL AND TESTAMENT of _____
was signed and declared to be his/her LAST WILL AND TESTAMENT in our presence at his/her request
and in his/her presence and the presence of each other as witnesses this _____

day of _____ , 19 _____ .

_____
(Witness signature)                                   (Address)

_____
(Witness signature)                                   (Address)

_____
(Witness signature)                                   (Address)

Page _____ of _____

# WILL
# SELF-PROVING CERTIFICATE

State of _____

County/City of _____

Before me, the undersigned authority, on this day personally appeared

_____
*Testator*

_____
*Witness*

_____
*Witness*

_____
*Witness*

known to me to be the Testator and Witnesses, respectively, whose names are signed to the attached or foregoing instrument and, all of these persons being by me first duly sworn, _____ _____ , the testator, declared to me and to the witnesses in my presence that said instrument is his/her LAST WILL AND TESTAMENT and that he/she had willingly signed or directed another to sign the same for him/her, and executed it in the presence of said witnesses as his/her free and voluntary act for the purposes therein expressed; that said witnesses stated before me that the foregoing will was executed and acknowledged by the testator as his/her LAST WILL AND TESTAMENT in the presence of said witnesses who, in his/her presence and at his/her request, and in the presence of each other, did subscribe their names thereto as attesting witnesses on the day of the date of said will, and that the testator, at the time of the execution of said will was over the age of eighteen years and of sound and disposing mind and memory.

_____
*(Testator signature)*

_____
*(Witness signature)*

_____
*(Witness signature)*

_____
*(Witness signature)*

Subscribed, sworn and acknowledged before me by _____ , the Testator,

and subscribed and sworn before me by _____

_____

_____ , Witnesses,

this _____ day of _____ , 19 _____ A.D.

Signed: _____
Notary Public
My Commission Expires: _____

(Seal)

# WILL
# SELF-PROVING CERTIFICATE

State of _____

County/City of _____

Before me, the undersigned authority, on this day personally appeared

_____
*Testator*

_____
*Witness*

_____
*Witness*

_____
*Witness*

known to me to be the Testator and Witnesses, respectively, whose names are signed to the attached or foregoing instrument and, all of these persons being by me first duly sworn, _____ _____ , the testator, declared to me and to the witnesses in my presence that said instrument is his/her LAST WILL AND TESTAMENT and that he/she had willingly signed or directed another to sign the same for him/her, and executed it in the presence of said witnesses as his/her free and voluntary act for the purposes therein expressed; that said witnesses stated before me that the foregoing will was executed and acknowledged by the testator as his/her LAST WILL AND TESTAMENT in the presence of said witnesses who, in his/her presence and at his/her request, and in the presence of each other, did subscribe their names thereto as attesting witnesses on the day of the date of said will, and that the testator, at the time of the execution of said will was over the age of eighteen years and of sound and disposing mind and memory.

_____
*(Witness signature)*

_____          _____
*(Testator signature)*                        *(Witness signature)*

_____
*(Witness signature)*

Subscribed, sworn and acknowledged before me by _____ , the Testator,

and subscribed and sworn before me by _____

_____ , Witnesses,

this _____ day of _____ , 19 _____ A.D.

Signed: _____
Notary Public
My Commission Expires: _____

(Seal)

# WILL
# SELF-PROVING CERTIFICATE

State of _____

County/City of _____

Before me, the undersigned authority, on this day personally appeared

_____
*Testator*

_____
*Witness*

_____
*Witness*

_____
*Witness*

known to me to be the Testator and Witnesses, respectively, whose names are signed to the attached or foregoing instrument and, all of these persons being by me first duly sworn, _____ _____ , the testator, declared to me and to the witnesses in my presence that said instrument is his/her LAST WILL AND TESTAMENT and that he/she had willingly signed or directed another to sign the same for him/her, and executed it in the presence of said witnesses as his/her free and voluntary act for the purposes therein expressed; that said witnesses stated before me that the foregoing will was executed and acknowledged by the testator as his/her LAST WILL AND TESTAMENT in the presence of said witnesses who, in his/her presence and at his/her request, and in the presence of each other, did subscribe their names thereto as attesting witnesses on the day of the date of said will, and that the testator, at the time of the execution of said will was over the age of eighteen years and of sound and disposing mind and memory.

_____
(Witness signature)

_____
(Testator signature)

_____
(Witness signature)

_____
(Witness signature)

Subscribed, sworn and acknowledged before me by

_____ , the Testator,

and subscribed and sworn before me by_____

_____ , Witnesses,

this _____ day of _____ , 19 _____ A.D.

Signed: _____
                    Notary Public
My Commission Expires: _____

(Seal)

# WILL
# SELF-PROVING CERTIFICATE

State of _____

County/City of _____

Before me, the undersigned authority, on this day personally appeared

_____
*Testator*

_____
*Witness*

_____
*Witness*

_____
*Witness*

known to me to be the Testator and Witnesses, respectively, whose names are signed to the attached or foregoing instrument and, all of these persons being by me first duly sworn, _____ _____ , the testator, declared to me and to the witnesses in my presence that said instrument is his/her LAST WILL AND TESTAMENT and that he/she had willingly signed or directed another to sign the same for him/her, and executed it in the presence of said witnesses as his/her free and voluntary act for the purposes therein expressed; that said witnesses stated before me that the foregoing will was executed and acknowledged by the testator as his/her LAST WILL AND TESTAMENT in the presence of said witnesses who, in his/her presence and at his/her request, and in the presence of each other, did subscribe their names thereto as attesting witnesses on the day of the date of said will, and that the testator, at the time of the execution of said will was over the age of eighteen years and of sound and disposing mind and memory.

_____
*(Testator signature)*

_____
*(Witness signature)*

_____
*(Witness signature)*

_____
*(Witness signature)*

Subscribed, sworn and acknowledged before me by _____ , the Testator, and subscribed and sworn before me by _____

_____ , Witnesses,

this _____ day of _____ , 19 _____ A.D.

Signed: _____
Notary Public

My Commission Expires: _____

(Seal)

# CODICIL

I, _____ , resident

of the _____ of _____ in the State of

_____ , being of sound mind, do make and declare this codicil to

be my LAST WILL AND TESTAMENT dated _____ , 19 ____ and

certify that I am not acting under undue influence, duress or menace.

In all other respects I ratify and confirm my Will and in witness whereof, I have hereunto set

my hand this _____ day of _____ , 19 ____ .

_____
*(Testator signature)*

This codicil to the LAST WILL AND TESTAMENT of _____

was signed and declared to be his/her codicil to his/her LAST WILL AND TESTAMENT in our presence

at his/her request and in his/her presence and the presence of each other as witnesses on this _____

_____ day of _____ , 19 ____ .

_____              _____
*(Witness signature)*                                                      *(Address)*

_____              _____
*(Witness signature)*                                                      *(Address)*

_____              _____
*(Witness signature)*                                                      *(Address)*

# CODICIL

I, _____ , resident

of the _____ of _____ in the State of

_____ , being of sound mind, do make and declare this codicil to

be my LAST WILL AND TESTAMENT dated_____ , 19 _____ and

certify that I am not acting under undue influence, duress or menace.

In all other respects I ratify and confirm my Will and in witness whereof, I have hereunto set

my hand this _____ day of _____ , 19 _____ .

_____
*(Testator signature)*

This codicil to the LAST WILL AND TESTAMENT of_____

was signed and declared to be his/her codicil to his/her LAST WILL AND TESTAMENT in our presence

at his/her request and in his/her presence and the presence of each other as witnesses on this_____

_____ day of _____ , 19 _____ .

_____
*(Witness signature)*                              *(Address)*

_____
*(Witness signature)*                              *(Address)*

_____
*(Witness signature)*                              *(Address)*

# CODICIL
# SELF-PROVING CERTIFICATE

State of _____

County/City of _____

Before me, the undersigned authority, on this day personally appeared

_____
*Testator*

_____
*Witness*

_____
*Witness*

_____
*Witness*

known to me to be the Testator and Witnesses, respectively, whose names are signed to the attached or foregoing instrument and, all of these persons being by me first duly sworn, _____ _____ , the testator, declared to me and to the witnesses in my presence that said instrument is a codicil to his/her LAST WILL AND TESTAMENT dated _____ , 19 _____ , and that he/she had willingly signed or directed another to sign the codicil for him/her, and executed it in the presence of said witnesses as his/her free and voluntary act for the purposes therein expressed; that said witnesses stated before me that the foregoing codicil was executed and acknowledged by the testator as a codicil to his/her LAST WILL AND TESTAMENT in the presence of said witnesses who, in his/her presence and at his/her request, and in the presence of each other, did subscribe their names thereto as attesting witnesses on the day of the date of said codicil, and that the testator, at the time of the execution of said codicil was of sound and disposing mind and memory.

_____
*(Witness signature)*

_____        _____
*(Testator signature)*                  *(Witness signature)*

_____
*(Witness signature)*

Subscribed, sworn and acknowledged before me by

_____ , the Testator,

and subscribed and sworn before me by_____

_____

_____ , Witnesses,

this _____ day of _____ , 19 _____ A.D.

Signed: _____
Notary Public
My Commission Expires: _____

(Seal)

# CODICIL
# SELF-PROVING CERTIFICATE

State of _____

County/City of _____

Before me, the undersigned authority, on this day personally appeared

_____
*Testator*
_____
*Witness*
_____
*Witness*
_____
*Witness*

known to me to be the Testator and Witnesses, respectively, whose names are signed to the attached or foregoing instrument and, all of these persons being by me first duly sworn, _____ _____ , the testator, declared to me and to the witnesses in my presence that said instrument is a codicil to his/her LAST WILL AND TESTAMENT dated _____ , 19 _____ , and that he/she had willingly signed or directed another to sign the codicil for him/her, and executed it in the presence of said witnesses as his/her free and voluntary act for the purposes therein expressed; that said witnesses stated before me that the foregoing codicil was executed and acknowledged by the testator as a codicil to his/her LAST WILL AND TESTAMENT in the presence of said witnesses who, in his/her presence and at his/her request, and in the presence of each other, did subscribe their names thereto as attesting witnesses on the day of the date of said codicil, and that the testator, at the time of the execution of said codicil was of sound and disposing mind and memory.

_____
*(Testator signature)*

_____
*(Witness signature)*

_____
*(Witness signature)*

_____
*(Witness signature)*

Subscribed, sworn and acknowledged before me by _____ , the Testator,

and subscribed and sworn before me by_____

_____

_____ , Witnesses,

this _____ day of _____ , 19 _____ A.D.

Signed: _____
Notary Public
My Commission Expires: _____

(Seal)

# LETTER OF INSTRUCTIONS

# LETTER OF INSTRUCTIONS